SAVE ME THE PLUMS

RANDOM HOUSE | NEW YORK

SAVE
ME
THE
PLUMS

My Gourmet Memoir

RUTH
REICHL

Published in the United States by Random House, an imprint and division of Penguin Random House LLC, New York.

RANDOM HOUSE and the HOUSE colophon are registered trademarks of Penguin Random House LLC.

Grateful acknowledgment is made to New Directions Publishing Corporation for permission to reprint the poem "This Is Just to Say" from THE COLLECTED POEMS: VOLUME I, 1909–1939 by William Carlos Williams, copyright © 1938 by New Directions Publishing Corporation. Reprinted by permission of New Directions Publishing Corporation.

Photograph on page xiii by Ernst Reichl.

LIBRARY OF CONGRESS CATALOGING-IN-PUBLICATION DATA
Names: Reichl, Ruth, author.
Title: Save me the plums : my *Gourmet* memoir / Ruth Reichl.
Description: New York : Random House, [2019]
Identifiers: LCCN 2018025584| ISBN 9781400069996 |
ISBN 9780679605232 (ebook)
Subjects: LCSH: Reichl, Ruth. | Food writers—United States—Biography. |
Gourmet.
Classification: LCC TX649.R45 A3 2019 | DDC 641.5092 [B]—dc23
LC record available at https://lccn.loc.gov/2018025584

Printed in the United States of America on acid-free paper

randomhousebooks.com

9 8 7 6 5 4 3 2 1

First Edition

Book design by Susan Turner

For Laurie Ochoa, who has made every writer she's ever worked with look better, and Jonathan Gold, who blazed a path for an entire generation of food writers. I couldn't have done it without you.

I have eaten
the plums
that were in
the icebox

and which
you were probably
saving
for breakfast

Forgive me
they were delicious
so sweet
and so cold
—WILLIAM CARLOS WILLIAMS,
"This Is Just to Say"

CONTENTS

AUTHOR'S NOTE

For almost seventy years *Gourmet* magazine chronicled American food, and it has an important place in our shared history. I can't know what the magazine meant to you, but if you're reading this, I assume *Gourmet* touched your life. This is the story of how it shaped mine.

SAVE ME THE PLUMS

MAGIC DOOR

I WAS EIGHT YEARS OLD WHEN I FIRST FOUND THE MAGAZINE, SIT-
ting on the dusty wooden floor of a used-book store. My father
was a book designer who enjoyed the company of ancient vol-
umes, and he often took me on book-hunting expeditions around
New York, leaving me with a pile of vintage magazines while he
went off to prowl among the dark and crowded shelves. That day
I picked up a tattered old issue of *Gourmet*, enchanted by the cover
drawing of a majestic swordfish leaping joyfully from the water.
This looked nothing like the ladies' magazines my mother favored, with their recipes for turkey divan made with cans of mushroom soup, or pot roast topped with ketchup, and I opened it to
find the pages filled with tales of food in faraway places. A story
called "Night of Lobster" caught my eye, and as I began to read,
the walls faded, the shop around me vanishing until I was sprawled
on the sands of a small island off the coast of Maine. The tide was

coming in, water tickling my feet as it crept across the beach. It was deep night, the sky like velvet, spangled with stars.

Much later I understood how lucky I was to have stumbled on that story. The author, Robert P. Tristram Coffin, was the poet laureate of Maine and a Pulitzer Prize winner with such an extraordinary gift for words that I could hear the hiss of a giant kettle and feel the bonfire burning as the flames leapt into the night. The fine spicy fragrance of lobster was so real to me that I reached for one, imagined tossing it from hand to hand until the shell was cool enough to crack. The meat was tender, briny, rich. Somewhere off in the distance a fish splashed, then swam silently away.

I closed the magazine, and the real world came into focus. I was a little girl leafing through the pages of a magazine printed long before I was born. But I kept turning the pages, enchanted by the writing, devouring tales of long-lost banquets in Tibet, life in Paris, and golden fruit growing on strange tropical trees. I had always been an avid reader, but this was different: This was not a made-up story; it was about real life.

I loved the ads for exotic ingredients you could send away for: oysters by the bushel, freshly picked watercress, alligator pears (avocados), and "frogs' legs from the frogland of America." Once I actually persuaded my parents to order a clambake in a pot from Saltwater Farm in Damariscotta, Maine. Eight live lobsters and a half peck of clams came swathed in seaweed and packed in ice. It cost $14.95, and all you had to do was poke holes in the top of the container and set it on the stove.

I couldn't get enough of those old issues, and now when Dad went off exploring bookstores I had a quest of my own. The day I discovered a battered copy of *The Gourmet Cookbook* among the ancient issues, I begged Dad to buy it for me. "It's only fifty cents," I pleaded.

It came in handy the morning I opened the refrigerator in our small kitchen and found myself staring at a suckling pig. I jumped back, startled, and then did what any sensible person would do: reached for the cookbook. I was only ten, and I hoped it would have some advice on how to deal with the thing.

Sure enough, there it was, on page 391: "Roast Suckling Pig Parisienne." There was even a handy photograph demonstrating how to truss the tiny animal.

I remember that moment, and not just because the recipe insisted on a lot of yucky stuff like putting a block of wood into the pig's mouth ("to brace it for the apple that will be inserted later") and boiling the heart for gravy. I remember it mostly because that was the day Mom finally admitted she was glad I'd found a hobby.

My mother's interest in food was strictly academic. Asked what had possessed her to purchase the pig, she replied, "I'd never seen one before," as if that was an adequate answer. The same logic had compelled her to bring home a can of fried grasshoppers, a large sea urchin with dangerously sharp spines, and a flashy magenta cactus flower. She had little interest in eating these items, but if I was going to insist on reading what she called "that ridiculous magazine," she thought it should be put to use.

The fried grasshoppers were not a hit; I suspect the can had been sitting on a shelf for years, awaiting some gullible customer. And while the editors were eager to instruct me in the preparation of eels, bears, woodchucks, and snipe, they were strangely silent on the subject of sea urchins. When I finally managed to pry the creature open, I found the gooey black inside so appalling that nothing would have tempted me to taste it. As for the cactus flower, its great good looks camouflaged a total lack of flavor.

But the suckling pig was a different story. I did everything the cookbook suggested and then hovered anxiously near the oven, hoping it hadn't led me astray. When the pig emerged all crackling skin and sweet soft meat, Mom was happy. "I've never tasted anything so delicious," she grudgingly admitted. "That magazine might be useful after all."

Dad took one bite and said, "Do you think you could figure out how to make Kassler rippchen?" There was a wistful note in his voice. "It was my favorite food when I was a boy."

"What is it?" I'd never heard of such a dish.

"Smoked pork chops. I imagine we could get them up in Yorkville."

I'd never been to Yorkville, but I knew Dad had lived there when he first arrived from Berlin in 1926. (He was twenty-six.) "You can't imagine how different it was from the rest of the city," he said as we rode the bus to the Upper East Side. "Every shop, every bakery, every restaurant was German, and in those first months I found it comforting to be surrounded by all those familiar sights and sounds."

I stared at my tall, rather formal father, fascinated by this glimpse into his past. Dad wasn't like American fathers—he didn't have pals, didn't go out drinking with the guys, had absolutely no interest in sports. I was his only child; he was almost fifty when I was born and was slightly baffled by this newfound fatherhood. Quiet, kind, and intellectual, he rarely talked about himself, and I was afraid if I uttered a single sound he would stop speaking.

"You know my grandmother was American," he said. I shook my head; I hadn't known that. "My grandfather came here in the middle of the last century, made a fortune, married an American, and carried her back to Germany. When I arrived in New York, all my grandmother's relatives came down to the boat to meet me. They wanted me to stay with them, but I felt more comfortable here. Oh, look!"

He'd spotted a butcher shop, its windows crammed with sausages in an astonishing array of shapes and sizes. We climbed off the bus, and as Dad opened the door we walked into a delicious aroma, all spice and smoke with a vague animal funk. I looked up; huge loops of sausage dangled from the ceiling, more kinds than I had ever imagined. There was another scent, something clean and briny that prickled my nose, and I followed the smell to a huge barrel of sauerkraut in the corner.

"Guten tag." I was shocked; I'd never heard Dad speak German before. But the unfamiliar language rolled off his tongue as he said, *"Leberkäse, landjaeger, bauernwurst,"* as if each word had a different flavor and he was savoring every one.

The butcher said something, pointing at me, and Dad shook his head. *"Schande."* The man tsked a bit as he handed a rosy slice of bologna across the counter. I put it on my tongue, tasting pork, celery seed, and something elusive and slightly sweet. Nutmeg?

"Zo kleine Madchen," the butcher said. "The father tells me you cook." He picked up a haunch of pork and sliced off a few thick chops. "Kassler rippchen is not difficult. They are smoked, so you have only to heat them up. *Und"*—he walked down the counter and filled a container with bright magenta strands—"a little red cabbage and just like that . . . a good German dinner."

Dad looked so happy as he pulled out his billfold and collected the parcels. "Would you like," he said almost shyly, "to explore another neighborhood next Saturday?"

That was how I came to love my native city. Dad and I began wandering the city's ethnic neighborhoods, discovering them through food. I loved La Marqueta, a tropical swirl of color that smelled of bananas, pineapples, and coconuts up in Spanish Harlem. Tito Puente's music was always playing as we moved through the crowded stalls, munching on fried plantains from a cuchifritos stand and ordering mofongo for the pure pleasure of saying the word.

Dad became almost garrulous on these walks, and I slowly

began to know him; once he took me to the Lower East Side, to Russ & Daughters, where I discovered that he had a passion for herring. "When your mother and I were dating," he said, "that's how she seduced me."

"But we never have herring!" I said.

"I know." He said it ruefully. "After we were married she confessed that she hates pickled fish. And she never bought it again." Another man would have been angry; Dad found it amusing, just one of life's little quirks.

What I was learning, on those weekend walks, is how much you can find out about a person merely by watching what he eats. Food became my own private way of looking at the world. But although it was my passion, I never thought of food as more than a hobby, and it never crossed my mind that it might be a way to earn my living. Even after college, when jobs proved elusive in the depressed New York of the early seventies and I began baking pastries for a restaurant called Food (run by a group of artists in the scruffy neighborhood that would come to be called SoHo), I considered it a stopgap measure, just something to do until my real life could begin.

Then a friend said, "You're such a good cook, you ought to write a cookbook," and everything changed. From the moment I picked up my pen, I knew that I had found my calling; I was twenty-two years old. *Mmmmm: A Feastiary* was not a big bestseller, but it made me a food writer. I moved to Berkeley, California, and although I continued to work in restaurants to pay the bills, I began contributing articles to magazines, working my way up from a small throwaway newspaper called *The East Bay Review of the Performing Arts* to *New West, Apartment Life,* and *Ms.* magazine. I dreamed of writing for the magazine that had set me on this path, but I lacked the courage to approach *Gourmet.* I was waiting for the perfect story.

It came to me in a spoonful of soup. Sitting in a small Thai restaurant, I ordered tom yum goong, which turned out to be the shocking pink of a Technicolor sunset. I took a tentative sip and suddenly there were fireworks in my mouth. Chilies, lemongrass, ginger, and cilantro exploded in waves of heat, cold, and sweetness. It was the most exciting food I'd ever tasted and I inhaled one spoonful after another, hoping the bowl would never end. I knew I had to go to Thailand and find out what real Thai food was like. This, I thought, is my *Gourmet* story. The next time I went to New York to see my parents, I made an appointment at the magazine.

The offices were just off Park Avenue, overlooking the Waldorf Astoria hotel. As a proud Berkeley person I found the formality intimidating, and all I remember about the editor who agreed to see me is that she was wearing white gloves and seemed terribly ancient. She took one look at my clothes—I was wearing my favorite hand-crocheted green chenille suit—shuddered slightly, and offered a limp handshake.

But she listened politely as I made my pitch. Brimming with energy, enthusiasm, and all the naïve earnestness of a young writer, I cried, "Thai food is going to be the next big thing."

"But our readers"—her voice was cool and distant—"have no interest in the next big thing. Other publications attempt to be timely; here at *Gourmet* we like to think of ourselves as timeless."

"That can't be true!" I replied. "I've learned everything I know about the food of other countries from the pages of your magazine. *Gourmet* has taken me to Mexico, China, India. . . . Now you need to take your readers to Thailand."

She regarded me with what I can only call pity. "We ran a story about food in Thailand a few years ago," she said.

"But you only wrote about Bangkok!" I protested. I did not point out that the article had been written by an expat surrounded by servants and living in regal splendor. Instead, I temporized. "It's a big country, and the food varies enormously from region to region."

The editor remained unmoved. "Thank you for taking the time to visit," she said.

I had been dismissed. Utterly crushed, I left the office.

Other magazines proved more enthusiastic, and I sold enough stories to be able to spend a month in Thailand pursuing unfamiliar flavors in the far corners of the country. I wished the articles were for *Gourmet,* but now when I picked up the magazine I saw that the adventurous spirit that had thrilled me as a child was gone. We had grown apart. I belonged to the rock-and-roll generation, thrilled by the changes in the American way of eating. *Gourmet* was a stately grande dame, looking admiringly across the ocean and wistfully back to the past.

The recipes were still reliable, but the tone had changed. Instead of stories about men rowing out for midnight lobster raids, there were prissy pieces about pricey restaurants and fancy resorts. I moved on to younger magazines, and although I continued to follow a few favorite writers (Laurie Colwin, Madhur Jaffrey, Joseph Wechsberg), for the next twenty-five years I rarely gave the magazine a thought.

2

TEA PARTY

THE PHONE WAS RINGING AS I FUMBLED FOR MY KEYS, ARMS FILLED with mistletoe and fir. I dropped the branches on the floor, pushed the door open, dashed into the apartment, and sprinted down the hall.

"Is this the restaurant critic of *The New York Times*?" The voice on the other end of the line had a British accent. "I am James Truman."

"Yes?" The name meant nothing to me.

"Editorial director of Condé Nast? I'd like to talk to you about *Gourmet*."

"*Gourmet*?"

"I am hoping," he went on, "that you will be willing to meet me for tea at the Algonquin. I'd ask you to the office, but we don't want the press to know we've been talking."

"The press?" What could that possibly mean?

"But he didn't give me a clue," I complained to my husband later. "All he would say was that he wants to talk. What do you think it's about?"

"They're probably looking for a new restaurant critic," Michael said reasonably.

It was the obvious answer. "I wouldn't write for them now," I said. "They're way too stuffy. So what's the point?" Even after two decades, just thinking about the half hour I'd spent in *Gourmet*'s office could make me wince. "I think I'll cancel the meeting."

"Go," said Michael. "You should find out what he wants. You may not be curious, but I certainly am."

Here's what I knew about Condé Nast before I sat down with James Truman: very little. I was aware that the company was owned by a strange and mercurial billionaire named Si Newhouse, who had recently sold Random House to Bertelsmann, a German media company—but I knew that only because they'd just published my first memoir. I knew that Condé Nast stood for luxury, class, and fashion and owned a lot of high-end magazines, but I was so oblivious I hadn't even known they'd bought *Gourmet*. (Given that I'd been a food critic for twenty years, that undoubtedly says a lot about me.) Two days later, when I walked into the restaurant of the Algonquin Hotel (famous for being the scene of Dorothy Parker's Round Table), I inhaled the scent of roasted beef, hothouse flowers, and nostalgia and wondered what I was doing there.

I followed the hostess through the dark, stubbornly old-fashioned room toward a pudgy, well-dressed gentleman seated alone at a large table. He, of course, would be my date. But the hostess kept walking, leading me to another table, where a scrap of a man rose to greet me.

Surprised, I took in the waiflike James Truman, who looked far too young to be editorial director of the vast Condé Nast empire. Could this man really be in charge of *Vogue*? His hair needed cutting and his rumpled clothes looked like he'd slept in them; whatever nervousness I'd had vanished.

I sat down to a table set for tea and Truman poured. "What do you think of *Gourmet*?"

Anticipating standard introductory small talk, I was caught off guard. And so I simply told the truth. "I went to the library yesterday to look through the last few issues, and . . ." I groped for a kind way to say this.

"And?"

"I'm sorry, but they put me to sleep. They're so old-fashioned; you'd never know this was 1998."

He seemed to be nodding agreement, so I forged ahead. "*Gourmet* is an important magazine, and it deserves better." I thought back to "Night of Lobster," which had so enthralled me as a child. "It used to be filled with such great writing; I remember reading M.F.K. Fisher and Annie Proulx in old issues. And did you know Ray Bradbury's *Dandelion Wine* first appeared in *Gourmet*? But now, just when the world is starting to get interested in food, you're publishing articles about Louis Vuitton tennis-ball holders!"

I'd noticed that in a recent issue and it struck me as the perfect example of everything that was wrong with the magazine. Truman did not react; apparently he didn't find it as ridiculous as I did. "As far as I can tell"—I tried to make the point—"*Gourmet* has become a place for rich people to plan their vacations."

Truman sat back a bit, and it occurred to me that he was trying to put some distance between us. Suddenly embarrassed, I toyed with my teacup, trying to gather my thoughts. "You must think I have a lot of nerve. I spend my life telling rich people where to eat, and here I am criticizing your magazine for doing the same thing. But being a restaurant critic often makes me uncomfortable. . . ."

"Why?"

"There are so many other food issues to write about!" I could feel myself climbing up on my high horse as I began ticking off subjects that interested me: the loss of farmland, disappearing fish, genetic modification, overuse of antibiotics. . . . "A couple of years ago I wrote a piece for *The New York Times Magazine* called 'Why I Disapprove of What I Do.'"

"I know; I read it."

My head jerked up in surprise. "You did?"

Truman flashed me an impish smile. "That's why I called; I thought it was interesting. I especially like the part where you said going out to eat used to be like going to the opera but that these days it's more like going to the movies. I thought then that you would make an excellent editor in chief for *Gourmet*."

I dropped my spoon, and it clattered against the thin porcelain. We both watched it vibrate against the saucer. Shocked, I said, "Editor in chief?"

"What did you think?"

"Well, I certainly didn't think you'd offer me a job like that!" He grimaced; I'd raised my voice. "I was thinking you probably wanted a new restaurant critic."

He looked so pained that I realized the man in charge of nineteen magazines didn't hire restaurant critics; he'd expected me to know he had something major in mind. But how could I possibly have imagined this? To cover my embarrassment I asked a question: "How many employees does *Gourmet* have?"

"I don't really know." He waved a hand at an invisible army of editors. "Sixty or so."

Sixty! The thought was terrifying. I couldn't possibly manage sixty people. Everybody has issues with the boss, and all I want to do is please people. "I'm no manager," I told him. "And I certainly couldn't handle a staff of sixty."

"Why not? You might have to clean house, get rid of everyone and bring in all your own people."

I almost laughed; where did he think I'd find these "people" of mine?

He must have read my face. "Human Resources would help," he said reassuringly. "That's what they're there for."

Clearly, he wasn't getting it. "Then there's the matter of budgets." I almost pulled out my checkbook to show him what a mess it was. "I'm terrible at managing money. What is *Gourmet*'s budget anyway?"

"I could get you that figure, but that's not really your concern." He sounded nonchalant. "You don't suppose Anna Wintour worries about budgets, do you? You'll have a managing editor to deal with money matters."

I didn't like his use of the future tense; he seemed to consider this a done deal. Didn't anyone say no to Condé Nast? "I suppose," I said with all the sarcasm I could muster, "this managing editor will be one of the new people I bring in after I 'clean house.'"

"Exactly!"

He had no idea who he was dealing with. I'd never fired a single person, even when I was an editor at the *Los Angeles Times,* and I certainly was not about to start now. I might be the restaurant critic of *The New York Times,* but at heart I was still a sixties rebel with a deep mistrust of corporate ways. My philosophy of management—if I had such a thing—would have gone like this: "Everybody's good at something. You just have to figure out what that is."

I stood up. "I'm flattered you've thought of me. I'm certainly not the obvious choice, and I wish that I could do it. But if you really want *Gourmet* to be the best it possibly can be, you need someone with experience."

Truman didn't move. "Think about it." He said it with confidence, as if he was sure I'd change my mind. I reached for my purse. "I'm pretty sure that if I were foolish enough to accept your offer, we'd both be sorry." Still he sat there, unmoving. What was he waiting for?

"Paparazzi," he mumbled, pointing toward the door as if he could see a phalanx of photographers waiting outside. "We don't want them to catch us leaving together."

I laughed out loud, finally understanding what those cryptic words on the phone had meant. Outside again, I looked around to see if there really were photographers lurking about. The sidewalk was empty; I wondered if Truman would be disappointed.

It took a full block before I realized that I had just turned down the chance to run the magazine that had inspired all the work I'd ever done. I began to wonder if I'd been rash.

Everything I'd told Truman was true: It was a watershed moment in American food and I yearned to do more than simply write about restaurants. That article about being ashamed of being a critic had been straight from the heart; in the back of my mind I always heard my mother's contemptuous voice saying, "Aren't you ever going to do something more important than tell people where to eat? Is this why we sent you to college?"

I thought too about my son. Nick was almost ten now and starting to complain bitterly about my working hours. He wanted a mother who was home at night to cook dinner and help with homework. It didn't seem like much to ask.

I'd spent nearly six years at the *Times,* and lately I'd been feeling it was time to move on. I loved my job and the people I worked with. We food reporters were a tight-knit group; we read one another's stories and cheered our colleagues on. And in my early days the editors had been remarkably protective of me; it was years before they let me know how controversial my first reviews of small Asian and Latino restaurants had been. "We didn't think you needed to know," they said. But I'd been writing restaurant reviews for more than twenty years, and few people last that long. Eating out fourteen times a week takes a toll on your body, and being away for most meals does not improve your family life. And after so much time on the restaurant beat I was eager for a challenge; I could practically write reviews in my sleep. That fall I'd brought this up so frequently that my friend Marion Cunningham insisted I visit her astrologer. "I know you don't believe in it," she said, "but whenever I'm at an impasse I visit Alex. It's always helpful. I'm making an appointment for you. My treat."

Feeling slightly silly, I'd actually gone to see the man. To my surprise, he told me things about myself I'd almost forgotten. He knew about the crippling panic attacks I'd finally overcome and my deep resistance to change. At the end of the reading, as he was putting his charts away, Alex looked up to offer a final thought. "The stars tell me that you're going to be getting a new job very soon."

"Do you know what it is?" I asked. "Do you know what I'll be doing next?"

He shook his head. "All I can tell you is that you are going to learn a great deal. And that it will completely alter your life."

3

GARLIC

"YES, YES, YOU TOLD ME ALL THAT." ON THE PHONE A FEW DAYS later, Truman sounded impatient. "I'm not asking you to take the job; I'm just asking you to talk with Si Newhouse. When we met I thought I was looking for an elegant dinner party, but you persuaded me that we should be asking for a great deal more. I'd like Si to hear your thoughts. Would you be willing to meet him for lunch?"

Conflicting emotions coursed through me. I was flattered: Truman thought Si Newhouse would be interested in my opinion. Also curious: After my tea with Truman, I'd read up on Newhouse, and I was intrigued. He spent millions on his magazines and never seemed to count the cost. Would he, I wondered, be willing to buy the best writers for *Gourmet*? Would he really allow the magazine to be more than an "elegant dinner party"? I have to admit too that, despite my skepticism about the occult, I couldn't get the astrologer's words out of my mind.

Now, watching Si shamble through the celebrities at the city's most expensive trattoria, Da Silvano, curiosity was winning. No one, I thought, would have taken him for one of the world's richest men. The great media mogul was small, wizened, and dressed in an ugly olive-drab sweatshirt. He had a long, horsey face and gaps between his teeth. When I stood to greet him, he motioned me down with jerky little gestures of the hand.

"Tell me . . ." he said with slow deliberation, parceling out the words as if each one was precious, "what you think of the recipes in *Gourmet*."

Recipes? Anticipating a lively discussion about the future of food magazines, I'd come armed with ideas.

"I don't cook much anymore," I replied. "I eat out fourteen times a week."

His face fell, and he looked so dejected that I thought, oh, what the hell. "I did take a look at the recipes last week," I admitted, "and I certainly wouldn't make most of them. They struck me as a bit lifted-pinkie. In my opinion they should come down to earth."

"Exactly!" The word rushed eagerly from his mouth, and I saw this was the answer he'd been hoping to hear. "My cook tells me they're too complicated."

To my horror, I groaned. He looked at me curiously. "And right there," I explained, "you have the problem."

"The problem?" His face had taken on the wary look of a child who fears he's about to hear something he'd rather not.

"Your magazine is printing recipes for people who have cooks! That might have been fine in 1941, but these days only people like you have cooks. *Gourmet* is living in the past."

Si recoiled, and I realized I might just have implied that he was old. I felt my face flush as I started casting around for something to say, venturing a few thoughts about the American food scene. Si appeared superbly uninterested, and after a few awkward attempts I gave up. He seemed to feel no obligation to keep the conversation afloat, staring across the table as if expecting to be entertained. The awkward silence stretched; I've never been much at small talk and I wished I hadn't come.

With great relief I saw the waiter approaching our table. He was bearing a large antipasto platter, but as he set it down Si eyed the dish suspiciously. His nose twitched. "Is there garlic in there?" he demanded.

"Yes, sir!" The waiter said it with pride.

"I can't eat garlic." Si waved an imperious hand. "Take it away."

The waiter looked agitated. "Sir"—he drew himself up—"does that mean the kitchen must avoid garlic in *everything*?"

Si gazed serenely up at him. "I told you," he said sweetly, "I cannot eat garlic."

The waiter remained rooted, not quite knowing what to do. I studied Si. When he'd suggested Da Silvano I'd been charmed; I'd recently reviewed the restaurant, saying how much I liked it, and it had seemed like an extremely gracious gesture. But now it struck me that an Italian restaurant was a strange choice for a man who shunned garlic. How would the chef manage? Would he even try? Si waved at the plate again and the waiter reluctantly picked up the rejected offering. I watched him hesitate outside the kitchen door, shoulders hunched in despair. He was, I knew, steeling himself for the chef's wrath.

In 1998, unlike today, restaurants did not routinely ask if you had allergies they should know about, and most were oblivious to such requests. Now I turned to Si and asked, "Don't you worry that the kitchen will try to sneak some garlic into your food?"

Si regarded me as if I'd said something stupid. "No," he said at last.

It was my turn to stare. I'd spent years dining out with anxious allergics who, not content to arrive at restaurants armed with gluten sensors, EpiPens, and caffeine monitors, peppered the waiter with excruciating questions. Looking at Si's complacent face I realized: Here was a man who was certain he'd get his own way.

As if to prove it, he said proudly, "Wait until you see the cafeteria Frank Gehry designed for our new offices!" His voice swelled with pride. "He's never built anything in New York before, and I had a hard time persuading him to do it."

Not that hard, I thought cynically; the Condé Nast cafeteria at 4 Times Square was rumored to be costing more than thirty million dollars.

"And," Si continued proudly, "George Lang, of Café des Artistes, will personally oversee the menu."

"Will they"—I couldn't resist it—"be serving garlic?"

"Of course not!" He seemed genuinely shocked. "I have stipulated that no garlic will ever be served in the Condé Nast cafeteria."

My mouth dropped open. I couldn't wait to tell Michael and Nick. What else, I wondered, had this eccentric man banished from his kingdom? Carnations? Trench coats? The color purple? How strange working for him must be: I imagined him decreeing that my hair was too curly and must immediately be cut, or that *Gourmet* should devote an entire issue to bacon or some other favored ingredient. I was positive now: I did not want the job.

Relieved, I lost myself in the food, concentrating on my cuttlefish. Charred until it puffed up like a tiny zeppelin, it was slicked with olive oil, sparked with bits of arugula, and sprinkled with copious amounts of garlic. From across the table, Si glared at my plate. I was beyond relieved when the interminable lunch ended.

Outside, a chauffeur stood waiting by a black sedan. "Get in," said Si. "Let me give you a ride."

"No need." Eager to escape, I pointed up the street toward the subway.

"You *can't* take the subway!" Genuinely appalled, Si practically pushed me into the backseat. The traffic was terrible, and as we fought our way up Sixth Avenue the silence became so oppressive that I almost jumped out of my skin. He hadn't asked a single question about any of the things I'd discussed with James Truman, and when I'd tried to bring them up, he'd put me off. What was I doing here?

Emboldened by frustration, I blurted out, "Why did you ask me to lunch?"

He eyed me coldly. Once again I had the impression that he considered the question rather stupid.

"James Truman said you wanted to discuss the future of food magazines." God, that sounded pretentious! I wished I'd kept my mouth shut. Besides, who did I think I was? What did I know about running food magazines?

For a full minute, Si did not respond. At last he said, "My friends in Los Angeles tell me that you are a wonderful editor."

"Editor? I'm a restaurant critic."

"But before you came to *The New York Times* you edited the food section of the *Los Angeles Times*. Have I got that right?"

I nodded, amazed that he'd done such diligent research. In my experience, New York media people looked down on West Coast publications, and I honestly hadn't expected him to know about that.

"They say"—I thought again how stingy he was with words, how reluctantly he permitted them to leave his mouth—"that it was both excellent and original. My compliments. I want *Gourmet* to be the premier epicurean publication in the country, and I thought we should meet."

So Truman had tricked me? "I'm very proud of that food section," I said hastily, "but newspapers are not like magazines."

Si waved an airily dismissive hand. "As I understand it, the *Los Angeles Times* has its own test kitchen and photo studio?"

I thought about the small test kitchen with its two homey cooks; compared to the famously capacious *Gourmet* kitchens, with their many food professionals, the *L.A. Times* facility was a joke. As for the photo studio . . . In my mind's eye I saw *Gourmet*'s perennial caption: "Photographed in *Gourmet*'s studios." I imagined lights, cameras, action.

"And," he continued, "your section won many awards?"

"Yes," I admitted. "But that still doesn't mean I could run a magazine."

"Many people," he said stubbornly, "manage the transition. You've made a fine name for yourself at *The New York Times*. We are prepared to provide you with all the resources you require, and I am convinced you would make a remarkable magazine."

"And I am convinced"—I can be stubborn too—"that you are making a huge mistake. *Gourmet* is an important publication, and you should hire someone who knows what she's doing. That would not be me."

The oddest smile danced across his face, and I realized that he was, at last, enjoying himself. He was a negotiator who liked the action, and my recalcitrance made it that much more fun. This had become a contest, and he was not a man who liked to lose. His voice became a low seductive purr. "You really should consider it."

He sat back, quiet now, but I didn't think he was done with me. Indeed, when the chauffeur stopped the car and I began to climb out, Si lifted a hand to stop me. "I have the greatest respect for *Gourmet*." He gave me a soulful look. "I am determined to make it the finest magazine in its category. I feel certain that you are the one to do it. Please give this your utmost consideration."

4

WASHINGTON SQUARE

I WATCHED THE LIMO PULL AWAY FROM THE *TIMES*, WAITING UNTIL it was out of sight. Then I pulled my coat around me and headed down the street. I think better when I'm moving.

Despite everything I'd said to Si, I had to admit that it was tempting. I thought back fifteen years, to when the *Los Angeles Times* asked me to be their restaurant critic. I had resisted then too, unwilling to leave the familiar comfort of Berkeley.

"You must go!" Mary Frances Fisher said when I told her of their offer. I'd become friends with America's most famous food writer while profiling her for *Ms.* magazine; we'd bonded over our mutual dislike of honey. Since then I'd gone to lunch at her Sonoma home every few months, thrilled by her attention. "You can't keep doing the same thing your entire life," she told me as she ladled out a bowl of split-pea soup liberally laced with sherry. "It's time you moved on, stopped playing it safe, took a chance. Working at a newspaper will give you some perspective. It's good for a writer to know that the words she's so carefully crafting today will be wrapping someone's fish bones tomorrow."

My Berkeley friends, however, had other ideas: To them this job meant selling out, and the people who shared my communal household were openly appalled. Even Alice Waters asked incredulously, "Are you really going to go work for corporate America?"

"Of course not," I said. What had I been thinking? I was a thirty-six-year-old freelance writer, getting by without a proper job or a weekly paycheck. Why would I give that up to go into an office and take orders? It wasn't me.

"I'm not sure you know who you really are, dear," Marion Cunningham said gently. I'd met the stunningly beautiful older woman at a party for James Beard (Marion was his West Coast assistant and had recently revised *The Fannie Farmer Cookbook*), and we'd instantly recognized that there was a bond between us. The next day I told her about the paralyzing panic attacks that kept me off bridges and freeways, and she confessed that agonizing agoraphobia had kept her prisoner in her house for years. She was forty-five before she overcame her phobias, but she'd sailed on into a bright and famous future; her *Breakfast Book* had been a huge bestseller. "You're making a mistake," she insisted. "Los Angeles"—like all older Angelenos, she pronounced the word with a hard "g"—"isn't a safe little sanctuary like Berkeley, but it's a real city and I know you will be happy there. Don't"—she leaned in to emphasize the point—"do what I did. Don't let your fears keep you from moving forward. It's such a sad waste."

Then Cecilia Chiang, who introduced sophisticated Chinese food to an American audience when she opened the Mandarin Restaurant, added her voice to the chorus. Cecilia is a force; even now, at ninety-eight, her energy remains undimmed, but back then she was a whirlwind with very decided opinions. In my early years as a food writer, she took me under her wing and became my Chinese tiger mother. "Of course you will take this job," she said in her elegant Shanghainese accent. "It is very prestigious. Don't even think of saying no."

These three formidable women could not have been more different, and the fact that they were speaking with one voice had a profound influence on me. The combined force of their opinions was too much to resist. I took the job.

I'd never regretted it, but Condé Nast was not the *Los Angeles Times*. In its heyday the newspaper was known as "the velvet coffin," a workplace so relaxed that reporters sometimes spent an entire year on a single story. Condé Nast, on the other hand, was a notorious pressure cooker filled with the most aggressive people in the business. Was I ready for that?

It was a cold day, and I huddled into my coat, listening to the voices in my head. Happy to lose myself in the anonymity of New York, I walked for a long time, leaning into the wind, unaware that I had a destination, until the Washington Square arch rose up before me.

I'd come home to Greenwich Village. To the large, solid building on the corner of 10th Street and Fifth Avenue that my parents had occupied for fifty years. They were both long gone, but I looked up at our old apartment on the eleventh floor, wondering what they would advise me to do.

Long ago, on a winter day like this, I'd come home from school to find Mom watching workmen hoist a large dead birch tree up to the eleventh floor. "It didn't fit in the elevator," she explained, "but isn't it wonderful? And such a bargain! I bought it on sale." She began to enumerate the many ways this improbable object was going to improve our lives.

Later, Dad and I came back down to this little patch of sidewalk to figure out how to deal with the huge object now occupying our living room. We always came outside to strategize over

Mom's more exotic purchases. We'd stood here for hours, in warmer weather, the day she announced she'd just bought a house in the country.

"You're going to love it!" she'd enthused. Mom was tall, with short iron-gray hair and a penchant for flamboyant clothes; I remember she was wearing a bright red shirtdress. "It's right on the water. And I bought a boat to go with it."

"A boat?" Dad ran his hands through his hair over and over, until the thatch covering his bald spot was standing straight up.

"A thirty-five-foot Chris-Craft cruiser we can park in front of our new house." Dad and I stared at each other in shock and terror; we knew from experience that there would be more. But all I could think to say was, "Mom, you don't park a boat. You anchor it."

Mom ignored this as she shifted into the aggressive tone she used at her most manic. By then we'd learned to read Mom's moods; after years on a psychiatrist's couch she'd finally been diagnosed as bipolar, and we'd come to expect the extreme swings that moved through her like weather, altering every aspect of her being. The doctors had yet to discover the drugs that could help her; one day she'd be a whimpering blob of self-doubt, the next a dictatorial titan determined to rule the world.

"Why *shouldn't* we have a nice home? I've also invested in a painting. It's a large abstract canvas—all blue and turquoise— that will look beautiful on the wall facing the water."

"Where did you buy this painting?" Dad's voice was unnaturally low, as soothing as one you'd use on a dangerous animal. I recognized this tactic; he was beginning to collect the information he'd need to undo the damage. We could not afford a single one of these things on a book designer's salary; together they were a financial disaster. Everything would have to go back.

Mom proffered a benign smile. "I met the *nicest* man on the bus the other day. He has a gallery on Fifty-seventh Street, and he suggested I stop in. When I saw my painting it felt like fate; it's just perfect for my house. Then, as I was leaving . . ." Mom stopped and for the first time faltered. Dad and I exchanged frightened glances; this was not a good sign. Something worse was coming.

"As you were leaving . . ." he prompted in that quiet voice. His face had taken on a papery, ashen hue. I felt sick.

"Well, it was Fifty-seventh Street, and there's that furrier right next door. What harm can there be, I thought, in stopping in? You know I've always wanted a mink coat."

"Oh, no!" The words escaped before I could stop them. I quickly covered my mouth; arguing with Mom when she was like this was a very bad idea.

She turned on me, furious, her voice rising in righteous indignation. "And why *shouldn't* I have a mink coat?" She stood up, then slammed her chair into the table. It reverberated, on and on, like the rumble of a drum.

"I wonder if there's anything else?" Dad whispered.

Haunted by the life she imagined for herself, Mom was constantly humiliated by the pedestrian reality of our existence. Dad worked hard but he never made much money, and our rent-controlled apartment was small. Mom liked to remind us that Bertrand Russell had once asked her to marry him, and although I thought she was exaggerating, she took me to meet him on his ninetieth birthday and it turned out to be true. The man she'd married instead—her first husband—had been wealthy, and although she'd married for love the second time, she tortured herself (and us) by making friends with fabulously rich people who owned giant apartments and vast country estates.

Even as a child I knew there was something pathetic about the way she made us dress up for cocktails at the Rainbow Room, the Forum of the Twelve Caesars, and the Top of the Sixes. We'd each order a single drink, stretching it out as long as possible. When we left, headed to dinner at the Automat, Mom would turn and stare longingly at the people in the dining room, wishing she were one of them.

She knew when every ocean liner came to town, and she'd make me and my best friend, Jeanie, dress up in our fanciest clothes so we could head down to the docks. In those days anyone could buy tickets to tour the great liners, and we'd board the *Île de France* or the *Queen Mary* and wander slowly through the luxurious staterooms, pretending we were there to see friends off. Afterward we'd stand on the pier, waving and shouting "Bon voyage!" until we were hoarse and the ship was gone. The wistful look on Mom's face was painful; she would have given anything to sail away.

Now, looking up at the apartment, it all came back to me. I never knew what to expect when I came home from school, and I'd stand outside the apartment door, key in hand, afraid to put it into the lock. Afraid of what was waiting on the other side.

I might open it to find the mom who was a ball of energy and sent me off on endless errands that needed to be done *right this minute*. Or the mom who'd wake me in the middle of the night, insisting that I clean the house. During these periods I'd hear her at midnight, still on the phone, planning parties, typing manuscripts, sending urgent letters to the far corners of the world. She'd spin ever-more-fantastic schemes. This could go on for months.

In one of her more manic moments, Mom rearranged our apartment. "Why waste space on bedrooms?" she cried, rousting Dad and me from our beds so she could send them to the Goodwill. "If we sleep on pullout sofas we can use every room to entertain." She threw parties, endless parties (in her manic moments she made friends with every stranger), so I never got enough sleep: Dessert was always served in my room.

Manic Mom ate nothing—she was too keyed up for food—

and she went on epic shopping sprees to buy new clothes, new furniture, new birch trees. Eventually she'd work herself into such a grandiose state that she'd pick fights with all her friends. And mine: Once, when Jeanie had the temerity to throw a tissue into the trash, Mom turned on her in fury. "Don't you *dare* put anything into my clean wastepaper basket!" she shouted at my trembling friend.

But inevitably the day would come when I'd arrive home from school to creepy quiet. Mom had gone to bed, where she would remain for months, reading the same book over and over (she was particularly fond of Vivien Leigh's biography), eating sweets, unable to rise from the sofa bed, which was now never closed.

When you have a bipolar parent, you never know what's coming. Change is always lurking, waiting to pitchfork you into a new life. You can't control it and you never know what form it will take. How I envied Jeanie, who could count on finding the same mother every time she came home. Like all children, I craved consistency; all I ever got was change.

During one of Mom's more manic episodes I asked Dad why he put up with it. Instead of replying, Dad went to his desk and returned carrying an old black-and-white photograph, curling at the edges, of a boy dressed in tails and a top hat. A huge medieval tapestry hung behind him; I could vaguely make out a unicorn. "Me," he said, "at about your age."

"Why are you wearing a costume?"

"It's not a costume; those are the clothes I wore when my governess took me downstairs to say good night to my parents. I grew up with all the things your mother dreams of."

"Even a boat?" I couldn't resist.

"Oh, yes." His smile was bitter. "My father was the commodore of the kaiser's yacht club. But I learned when I was very young that things can't make you happy. My parents' Berlin house was cold, and I couldn't wait to escape. All I ever wanted was to work with books, but the family didn't think that grand enough. That's why I came to America."

Dad loved books, loved them so much I'd sometimes enter a room to find him running his hands across the pages of the latest one he'd designed as if it were whispering secrets meant for him alone.

"Oh, Rusie . . ." When Dad was serious, his German accent grew more pronounced. "I often think that if your mother had work she loved, work that challenged her, she wouldn't want so much or do such crazy things. She's just bored and frustrated. It's so sad for her; she's a smart woman who was born at the wrong time."

It is a sign of how oblivious—or perhaps hopeful—my father was that he refused to accept how sick Mom was. But Dad truly loved the woman he had married, and he never stopped believing that if he could only find the magic bullet she would be cured.

He reached out and ran his fingers down my cheek, continuing the thought. "But I hope things will be different for you. The world is changing. What I want most for you is challenging work that makes you proud. It's the key to happiness."

Remembering his words, I realized that although he'd put it differently, this was exactly what Mary Frances, Marion, and Cecilia had told me the first time I'd been offered a new job. But now I heard a different message. What they were saying was that it wasn't the job that frightened me: I was just terrified of change. I heard Mary Frances saying, very clearly, "It's time you stopped playing it safe."

I'd come in search of an answer. And I'd found it. I took a final look up at the apartment where the last rays of winter sun were glinting off the windows. Then I turned and made my way uptown.

5

ATTIRE ALLOWANCE

"BEFORE YOU DECIDE TO TAKE THE JOB," MY AGENT, KATHY ROB-bins, said, "there's something you need to know about *Gourmet*." She paused, as if trying to figure out how to put it. And then: "The magazine's publisher is in the family."

"The family?"

"Si's family. Gina Sanders is married to Steven Newhouse, his nephew."

I didn't like the sound of that. "What you're saying is that if we ever had a fight, I'd lose."

"What I'm saying is, go meet her before you make a final deci-sion. Because if you don't get along, the job will be a nightmare."

Gina Sanders was only in her thirties, but on the phone she sounded oddly formal. When I asked how I'd know her, she re-plied, "I'm five foot three and I'll be wearing business attire."

Who uses the word "attire" in ordinary conversation? But the description proved useful: There was only one person in the coffee shop not dressed in casual clothing, and as I headed for her table I noted that the small woman in the conservative gray suit had shiny brown hair, bright eyes, and a pointed chin. I almost laughed: This was not the frightening businesswoman I'd envisioned. Gina Sanders made me think of a character in a children's book, a sleek little fox dressed in grown-up clothing.

She eyed me with some alarm. I was rather proud of my outfit; I'd recently discovered a vintage coat from the fifties in a thrift shop, and I loved the way it hugged me tightly to the waist before erupting into a swirl of velvet skirt. Gina, however, was clearly not impressed. It did not help that the melting snow on this blustery January morning had leaked through my old leather boots, which were emitting embarrassing little squeaks with each step. She looked down as I sloshed toward her, then quickly adjusted her face and held out her hand, fingers pointed downward.

"Thank you for coming down to the Village to meet me. I wanted to be sure we wouldn't be seen."

Did everyone at Condé Nast think they were being stalked by paparazzi?

She'd obviously expected someone older, more fashionable, and decidedly more formidable. As we made idle small talk, I could sense her questioning Si's judgment. She remained cool, even distant, until I mentioned that I'd grown up a few blocks away. At that, her entire demeanor changed. "My house is just around the corner!" she cried.

"Which one?" When I was small, Dad walked me up 10th Street every morning on the way to P.S. 41. He'd peer into the apartment windows we passed, inventing stories about the people who lived inside. He decided that the man who sat in the bow window, the one who waved whenever we walked by, was a retired sea captain. He made up fantastic adventures for the girl on the fourth floor who looked like Audrey Hepburn. But he didn't have to dream up stories about the family in what was now Gina's townhouse; they were old friends.

"Ruth Wittenberg was an amazing woman," I told Gina. "She fought for suffrage and civil rights, and she was a famous gardener. Your house was always the main feature on Village garden tours, but I was much more interested in the dining room: Phil collected cookbooks, and the floor-to-ceiling bookshelves were filled with them. Are they still there?"

Gina made an odd little face, as if she'd swallowed something bitter. "Nothing's still there. My mother-in-law had Mario Buatta decorate the house as a wedding present." She leaned in meaningfully, as if I'd empathize.

I didn't know anything about the decorator—or any decorator, for that matter—but back at the office I looked him up. Buatta favored heavy drapes, patterned fabrics, and overstuffed furniture—conventional comfort at its most luxurious. I thought it was a good sign that Gina didn't like his style; it seemed meant for older people.

"She seemed nice enough," I reported to Kathy, "but she struck me as very ordinary."

"Could you work with her?"

"I don't see why not. Although," I couldn't help adding, "I didn't get the impression she thought much of me."

"She must have liked you better than you think." Kathy's voice was brisk. "Because Condé Nast just called to make an offer. Do you want to hear the terms?"

Two minutes later I hung up in a daze. All around me the newsroom buzzed, familiar, cheerfully distracting. My fingers shook as I dialed to cancel the reservation at Les Celebrites, the fancy new restaurant I was supposed to be reviewing; Michael and I could not possibly discuss this in the middle of a packed room where we could be overheard. Then, still dizzy, I turned off my computer and picked up my purse.

I considered dinner as I rode the subway. I'd stop at Citarella to buy some shrimp, make that Marcella Hazan pasta Nick and Michael liked so much. I'd get a bottle of wine. A bunch of flowers. Bake brownies.

At home I stood in the kitchen, mind spinning as I stripped shells from the shrimp. In the living room Nick and his friend Zack were doing math homework. The murmur of their voices made this seem like any other day.

"You boys hungry?"

After years of insisting on five white foods, my son's appetites had abruptly changed; he was now on the constant prowl for interesting snacks. "Any more of those deviled eggs?" he shouted back.

I put the eggs on a plate and carried them into the living room; they were slightly smashed, which gave them a rakish air, but the boys didn't seem to mind. I'd finished cleaning the shrimp by the time Michael walked in, but I was still at the sink, my hands beneath the running water.

"Are we staying home tonight?" Michael opened the refrigerator, rooting around for a beer, an expression of pleasure on his face.

"Condé Nast made me an offer."

We'd already discussed the pros and cons; Michael thought I should stay at the *Times*. He mistrusted Condé Nast—the company was such a revolving door—and was convinced they were more interested in luring a writer away from the *Times* than in revamping the magazine. Despite Si's promises, Michael worried that once I got there he'd veto all substantial changes. "I just don't want you to be disappointed," he said.

He'd cheered me on at every move, urging me to take jobs at both the *Los Angeles Times* and *The New York Times,* and I trusted both his instincts and his judgment. If not for him, I'd still be in Los Angeles.

But he trusted my instincts too. "I haven't met the man. You have, and if you really believe Si Newhouse is going to let you make the magazine of your dreams, then you should probably take the job." He retrieved a Heineken and opened a drawer, searching for a bottle opener.

"Don't you want to hear their offer?" I gave him the figure.

His hands stilled. "Say that again."

I repeated the number.

"Are you sure you heard right? Six times what you're making now? Is that possible?"

We stood staring at each other across the open drawer, stunned by our naïveté; he was a producer at CBS and I'd worked at the country's biggest papers, but neither of us had ever known that journalists could earn that kind of money.

"I made Kathy repeat it twice. And that's not all. There's a driver. A car. A clothing allowance."

"A *clothing* allowance?" It came out halfway between a sputter and a snort. He had finally located the opener and I watched him open the beer and take a quick gulp.

"Apparently they pay for everything. Country clubs—"

"Can't you just see us in a country club?"

"—hairdressers, travel. You name it. It's kind of unreal. I worry about the money, worry it will change us."

Michael came to the sink, turned off the water, and put his arms around me. "If this is what you want to do, then you should go for it. It's risky, but you're fifty years old and if you're ever going to do it, now's the time."

"I'll probably make an enormous fool of myself."

"No, you probably won't."

"And then there's all that other stuff—like the sixty people I'm supposed to send packing."

"You don't have to."

"Don't have to what?" With a child's unerring instinct, Nick chose that moment to appear with the empty plate. He set it in the sink and looked up at me.

"Fire a lot of people."

"Oh." Nick's eyes went to Michael, knowing something was missing.

"Mom's just been offered a new job."

"You mean you wouldn't be a restaurant critic anymore?" Nick's voice rose, excited. "You wouldn't have to go out all the time? We could eat dinner at home? Every night?"

"Well, yes."

"Do it! Do it! Do it!"

6

PLAN CHECK

THREE MINUTES AFTER THE CONTRACT ARRIVED, THE PHONE RANG. When I picked up the receiver, a torrent of staccato screeches came pouring out. I held it far away from my ear, trying to decipher the words. At last I grasped that Condé Nast's PR czar was on the line. I had yet to meet Maurie Perl, but her rat-a-tat communication conjured up a large, fierce woman with dark hair and huge red lips. She finally ran out of steam and slowed down enough to make me understand that she was talking about the need to control the news.

"When," she said very slowly, as if speaking to someone of limited mental capacity, "were you planning to give notice at the *Times?*"

I had not given this a single thought. "I guess I'll tell my editor tomorrow morning."

An intake of breath. "Not your editor! You have to go right to the top."

"You want me to tell Lelyveld directly?" Joe Lelyveld was the executive editor of *The New York Times*.

"Of course!" A pause. "Now, we have to consider the timing. This is going to be very big and we want to be on top of it."

"It was so funny," I told Nick and Michael at dinner. "She has such an exaggerated sense of the importance of this."

"These are the people who think paparazzi are following them around," Michael reminded me.

"Well, I hope Maurie's not disappointed. I can't imagine many people are going to care, but she's treating it like a military operation. She's timed it to the last millisecond."

"Does she have a stopwatch?" Nick asked.

"I wouldn't be surprised. She's created a minute-by-minute timetable. I tell Joe. Then I call her. She calls Truman. He fires the current editor."

I didn't know Gail Zweigenthal, but I knew she'd been at *Gourmet* for her entire career and was, by all accounts, a very nice woman. I hoped this wasn't going to come as a terrible shock. I also hoped the rumors about Condé Nast's generosity were true and that she had a golden parachute (although there was no mention of such a thing in my contract).

"What then?" asked Nick.

"Then Maurie makes phone calls. She's very concerned about some guy named Keith Kelly, who's the *Post*'s media critic; she kept saying we have to give him an exclusive interview before the news leaks out. And she must have told me a thousand times that I'm not allowed to talk to *anyone* unless she says it's okay."

The next morning I made pancakes and watched Michael pack his suitcase. The Clinton impeachment hearings were in full swing, and he was off to Arkansas to work on yet another story. As an investigative producer for CBS, he was always on the road, following the story wherever it led. "I wish I didn't have to leave right now." He zipped the suitcase closed. "I'm sorry you're facing this alone."

Nick came in, bouncing the pink rubber ball he always kept in his pocket, and looked up at Michael. "Are you taking me to school?" There was a wistful note in his voice; he hated having either of us leave town.

Michael punched him lightly on the arm. "Don't look so sad, pal; it's only a few days."

Nick slipped his hand into Michael's and we all walked to the hallway to wait for the elevator. I felt queasy; everything was about to change. I hoped this wasn't a huge mistake.

THE DONUT MAN ON THE corner of 43rd Street and Broadway handed me coffee and a jelly donut; after six years, he knew exactly what I wanted. "Give me one for Stan too," I said. Kassim nodded; I often took coffee to my favorite guards. They, in turn, occasionally shared the giant sandwiches they bought at the Big Apple Meat Market on Ninth Avenue, which was famous for its overstuffed heroes.

"You're in early." Stan was a beefy, talkative man who loved telling me about his favorite restaurants on Staten Island. I was going to miss him, miss this little ritual that started every day.

I pushed through the security turnstile, wondering about the guards over at Condé Nast; thanks to the cloak-and-dagger manner in which we'd conducted our affair, I'd never been inside the building.

Upstairs, the style section was still empty and I looked around, taking in the details, already nostalgic. A tan cardigan sat sentinel at Alex Witchel's pristine desk, a warning to interloping freelancers that she might be right back. Elaine Louie's desk overflowed in its usual state of chaos. I watched a startled mouse leap across the jumbled papers and disappear beneath the desk Trish Hall used. The former editor of the dining section still came in from time to time; I hoped the mouse would be gone by the time she arrived. I was going to miss these people, miss the easy camaraderie with my colleagues; there was always someone to talk to, someone who'd come upstairs for a cup of coffee or go out for a bite to eat.

Gourmet would be different: Nobody wants to gossip with the boss. It must be unpleasant, I thought, to be surrounded by people who are afraid of you.

But even when Trish Hall was at her most powerful, she'd never thrown her weight around and never insisted she knew more than you did. She was also completely candid about wanting to work with people she could learn from. My first boss, Rosalie Wright, had been much the same. Rosalie is the toughest person I've ever met: She bucked enormous pressure to run major investigative articles in *New West*. When powerful people pulled strings and made threats as they attempted to stop the first negative stories about Jim Jones's Peoples Temple, she was fearless. "The story's solid and it's shocking," she said, refusing to give in. But Rosalie never pulled rank; if she was alone in the office, she'd take phone messages for you, and she was constantly saying, "You're the expert. What do you think?" Unlike the men I'd worked for, Rosalie managed to be in charge without ever being a boss. It came to me that I had excellent role models; I just had to keep them firmly anchored in my mind.

I called Joe's secretary, who promised to let me know the moment he arrived. Edgy and anxious, I occupied myself by taking down the papers pinned to the bulletin board above my desk. Phone numbers: Nick's pediatrician, the vet, various babysitters. A note from Mike Nichols, thanking me for taking him on a review. A snapshot of Nick standing upright on Michael's shoulders. It was ancient history: They stopped performing that trick the year Nick turned six.

The secretary called to say Joe would see me now, and I went downstairs, heart thumping as I entered his office. Joe looked up and uttered exactly two words. "Condé Nast?"

I nodded and his lips turned down.

Rumor had it that Joe was angry about Si poaching his people; Paul Goldberger had recently left to be the architecture critic of *The New Yorker*. "What will you be doing there?" he asked grimly.

"I'm going to edit *Gourmet*."

His expression quickly changed. "I can't blame you for being tempted by that." He was almost smiling. "It's a wonderful opportunity." Now it was actually a grin. "My wife's a longtime subscriber." Why was he so happy?

Suddenly I understood: He'd been afraid I was off to *The New Yorker*, *GQ*, or *Vanity Fair*. One of the *important* magazines. I sat up straighter. "Do *you* ever read *Gourmet*?" I asked.

He looked incredulous. "I don't have time for food magazines." The disdain in his voice was palpable.

"That's exactly why I took the job. I plan to make a magazine you'll *have* to have time for."

"I wish you luck" was all he said.

Back at my pod, I dutifully dialed Maurie. "Get out, get out," she commanded. "You don't want to answer questions from the *Times*. It would be best if you came here."

Condé Nast had not yet moved into the modern skyscraper that would transform Times Square from a derelict honky-tonk district into a squeaky-clean tourist attraction. The company occupied a venerable old edifice, which had started life in 1922 as the home of the Borden Company, but when Si moved his magazines in he'd given the place modern polish. As I walked east toward 350 Madison Avenue, leaving the still-gritty theater district behind me, the sidewalks became cleaner, the stores more elegant, the pedestrians better dressed. I passed Prada, Gucci, Chanel. Even the guards, I thought as I entered the lobby, looked classier at Condé Nast; their backs were straighter, their uniforms crisper, and there was not a paunch among them. As I waited for the elevator, someone who looked a lot like Graydon Carter strolled up. The editor of *Vanity Fair* fascinated me; he'd co-founded *Spy* magazine, where he'd invented wonderfully nasty nicknames for a host of people (Donald Trump was a "short-fingered vulgarian"), before transforming himself into a card-carrying member of the social elite. I studied him; with his wild mane and beautiful suit he reminded me of a superbly self-satisfied lion. In the research I'd been doing on Condé Nast, I'd learned that Graydon hired a private architect to design his office.

Maurie also fit so perfectly into this elegant atmosphere that the image I'd had of her instantly vanished. Blond and petite, dressed in cashmere, tweed, and diamonds, she reminded me of a miniature poodle fresh from the groomer. She placed the first call and to my discomfort stayed on the line, listening intently as I fielded questions from Keith Kelly. It was awkward having her listening in, but when I protested she insisted that this was common practice. One more reminder that I had just entered a new world.

Maurie dialed again, and again, and again; I hadn't known there would be so many interviews, but I seemed to be doing okay. She never interrupted as I sat for what felt like hours, talking to the press. Between calls she tried to reassure me, offering a smile as conspiratorial as a wink. Now that I was officially on board, she acted like we'd been friends forever.

Around midday Si's secretary called, and Maurie jumped as if a shot had been fired, manicured fingers making small shooing motions. "Go. Go. Go." There was that smile again. "Don't be afraid. Last time he called I was so terrified. Then I got to his office and it was worse: Steve Florio was there too! The owner and the CEO? I was *positive* I was being fired. And what did they do? Handed me the keys to a new car and thanked me for doing a good job." She walked me to the door, practically pushing me out.

But Si did not have cars on his mind. "I want you to come to *Gourmet*'s offices on Lexington Avenue tomorrow morning." The words, as always, emerged slowly, as if he could not bear to part with them. "The staff will want to meet you."

"But I don't start for three more months!" I'd agreed to stay at the *Times* while they sought my replacement, and as far as I was concerned the *Gourmet* job was off in the distant future. What was the point of meeting the staff now?

"Everyone in New York will be talking about this tomorrow! You must be introduced. It cannot wait."

I had not anticipated this. Then I thought of Maurie's time line and felt like a fool. The old editor of *Gourmet* was already gone; of *course* the staff would want to meet the new one.

OUTSIDE SI'S OFFICE ANOTHER ASSISTANT pounced; she had clearly been lying in wait. "Mr. Truman wonders if you have a few minutes for him?" She pointed to another door.

"There you are!" Truman was on his knees unrolling a large set of blueprints. "We'll be moving to Four Times Square in a few months"—he put one knee down to keep the blueprint flat—"but if we act fast there's still time to redesign your office."

Office. I'd never even considered that. The only office I'd ever had was a repurposed broom closet at the *L.A. Times,* and nobody had consulted me on décor.

"Gail designed her office, but of course you'll want something different."

I looked down at the blueprint, noting that the windows on the space marked GOURMET EDITOR'S OFFICE stretched up Broadway for the better part of a block. The office was the size of a loft! What on earth was I going to do with all that room? I liked the coziness of the pod I shared with four other reporters at the *Times,* liked being surrounded by the friendly buzz of conversation. It was good to be able to look up and ask, "Has anyone ever eaten alligator? Can you describe the taste?" Now I had a bleak vision of myself, all alone in my regal space. The least I could do, I thought, was make sure my door was always open.

A decorator appeared, arms laden with sample books. She spread them across Truman's desk, dealing them out like cards. The array of fabrics was so dizzying that it called to mind Gina talking about her mother-in-law's decorator. What, I wondered, would *her* office look like?

"Gail selected this wallpaper." The decorator pointed to a thick swatch of straw-colored fabric. "But of course you can have anything you want. Did you have a color scheme in mind?"

"I like bright colors."

"Oh, good." She seemed pleased. "Most of the editors stick to neutrals. Your office will be different." She began handing me photographs of desks, chairs, and lamps.

"What I really want," I confided, "is a big table where we can gather for meetings."

The decorator frowned. "You don't need a table; there's a conference room for that." She thrust more fabric samples at me. "This is your private office; you're going to need sofas."

"I want a table," I insisted. "I'll probably invite people in to lunch."

"There's a private dining room for that," she demurred.

"A private dining room?"

"Of course," she said nonchalantly. "*Gourmet* is a food magazine."

"Actually," Truman interjected, "the dining room belongs to the publisher. So if Ruth wants a table, she should have one."

"As you wish." She leafed resignedly through one of her books. "How's this?" She pointed to a large round table, light wood delicately balanced on slim polished legs; the price would have covered every stick of furniture I'd ever owned.

"Beautiful," I breathed.

The decorator scribbled something. "Do you like these chairs?"

They were beautiful too, a light buttery wood with red suede seats. She made another note and reached for a different book.

"Now," she murmured, presenting it to me, "let's discuss bathroom fixtures."

"I have my own bathroom?" An image of the ladies' room at the *Times* flashed through my head: The toilets leaked, the fluorescent lights hiccupped, and broken towel dispensers trailed paper across a cracked tile floor. "Does it have a shower?"

I'd meant it as a joke, but the decorator was apologetic. "I'm so sorry," she said, "but that's not in the plans."

ADJACENCIES

7

I STOOD AT HOME, IN FRONT OF THE MIRROR, REHEARSING THE speech. It was short and filled with bland platitudes, which I went over and over again in my mind as I rode the subway. I'm so excited about this opportunity! We're going to do great things together! What else could I possibly say? I wouldn't really start working at *Gourmet* until May.

The subway was crowded, the floor a slippery sludge of melting snow, the air steamy from all our wet wool coats. The man behind me was wearing an enormous backpack that kept jutting painfully into my ribs, no matter how much I squirmed about trying to keep from being poked. The woman sharing the metal pole with me had folded her newspaper lengthwise in a vain attempt to read it and my eye caught my name. REICHL GALLOPING . . . was all I could make out, no matter how I twisted and turned. It was hopeless.

Outside, I stopped at the first newsstand and bought a copy of the *Post*. And there it was—Keith Kelly's column. Maurie hadn't been so crazy after all.

Reichl Galloping to Run *Gourmet*

In yet another stunning editor shift at Condé Nast, *New York Times* restaurant critic Ruth Reichl has been tapped as the new editor in chief of *Gourmet*.

The 51-year-old critic, who takes great pains to guard her anonymity at the *Times*, will take over in April from Gail Zweigenthal, who is stepping down after 34 years with the magazine.

I scooped up all the other papers, but the only other mention I found was in an advertising publication. The editor of a competing food magazine was quoted as saying, "What does a restaurant critic know about running a magazine? We're going to eat her lunch."

Oh, great, I thought, we're off to a fine start.

GOURMET WAS STILL IN THE ugly brick skyscraper I'd visited so long ago, and as I pressed the elevator button I remembered the way the editor had sneered at my ideas. I exited to find an elegant blond receptionist who might be the very same woman who'd told me to take a seat back then, and when I gave my name she regarded me with similar disdain. "This," her face said very clearly, "is the new editor in chief?"

"They're waiting for you." She pointed through a glass door to a large sitting area, and I stood making nervous small talk with Si and Gina as the staff moved slowly into the room, jostling for a better view. They looked slightly shell-shocked, and they stared at me as Si began to speak, his soft voice making no concession to the size of his audience. We all leaned in to hear his words, which were punctuated by long pauses. "The mayor called to congratulate me this morning. Mayor Giuliani said the magazine's gain was the city's loss." He gazed around with a satisfied smile.

He went on to say a few more complimentary things and to underscore his high hopes for the future of *Gourmet*. Then he turned to me. "And now Ruth would like to say a few words."

I looked at their frightened, expectant faces, and the perfunctory speech I'd memorized vanished from my head. What an idiot I was! It hit me for the first time that not one of these people knew if they still had a job. "You might have to clean house," I heard Truman saying. They were terrified, and it was up to me to reassure them.

My mind went blank, and I began to be afraid I was going to have a panic attack. The nightmare of my first job interview suddenly came back to me—it was at *Esquire* magazine, just a few blocks from here, and I was sure I'd forgotten how to breathe. Dizzy and unable to focus, there was such a buzzing in my head that I almost passed out and completely blew the interview. Now my head was filled with the same sounds, and my heart was beating so loudly I was sure everyone could hear it. The silence became thick. People shifted awkwardly. I remember the sound of a fire truck racing down Lexington Avenue, sirens shrieking, and the way the blare filled the room.

I looked around, hoping to catch the eye of the one person I knew at *Gourmet;* it would be heartening to see a friendly face. But the magazine's executive food editor, Zanne Stewart, was nowhere in sight. The room was too warm. It was a nightmare. A bead of sweat began to inch its slow way down my back. And still I could not find a single word.

The room began to sway, and it occurred to me that I needed to breathe. Si shot me a worried look. Gina looked distressed.

I forced myself to open my mouth, praying a word would come out. Any word.

Finally I managed: "I'm very happy to meet you all."

A little frisson of relief zoomed around the room.

"This has all happened very quickly, and I know you're as stunned as I am."

There were nods. I must be making sense. Connecting.

"For the next few months"—they all leaned forward again, eager to hear their fate—"I'll continue to be the restaurant critic of *The New York Times.*"

An angry rumble traveled through the group. Heads swiveled. They looked at one another in undisguised horror. A few months? "But what about now?" Did someone really say that?

"In the meantime . . ." The room went quiet. "I hope to get to know you all. I want this magazine to be a group effort, something we create together, so although I'll still be working at the *Times,* I'll be coming in every day, trying to get started."

Had I really said I was going to do two jobs? I'd been hoping to please them, but it did not seem to be enough. They stood, unmoving, waiting for more.

"Please come by and introduce yourselves." I took a step backward to indicate that the show was over, crossing my arms so no one could see how badly my hands were shaking.

Si slipped away and Gina went to her office. Nobody else moved. At last a small round woman detached herself from the crowd. "I'm Robin." She tapped my arm. "I'm the editor's secretary. Would you like me to show you Gail's office?" She went red and quickly corrected herself. "I mean your office."

Unaware that she would be one of the most important people

in my new life, I followed Robin gratefully down a hall. She motioned to a door, and I went through to a large, bright, windowed room. She indicated the seat behind the solid wooden desk and waited while I sat down. Then we studied each other.

She was, I thought, aptly named: With her bright eyes, small round body, and tiny feet, she reminded me of a plump little bird. "I've been working at Condé Nast for twenty years," she chirped, "and I hope you aren't planning on bringing in your own secretary."

"I have no secretary." I tried to decipher the look that crossed Robin's face. There was relief but also something more elusive. Could it be triumph? Why?

Sporting a satisfied little smile, Robin began organizing the editors, leading them in one by one. They were polite. They were eager. They were desperately obsequious. But as they explained why they were all essential to the operation, my anxiety level rose.

"I'm very good at dealing with the teeosee," said the first editor. I stared at her, wondering if I should admit that I had no idea what she was talking about.

The next was even more mysterious. "I'm a wizard with inadequate sep," she announced. I felt a headache lodge itself behind my right eye. It did not help that I had a hard time telling them apart; they all seemed to be blond women with names ending in "y." "I kept telling Gail," said the next one—was she Hobby?— "that we need to enlarge our well."

I pounced on the soothingly familiar word. "I'll look into it," I promised. "Good water is so important to a cook." She looked confused, and I saw I'd gotten it wrong. Flustered and embarrassed, I tried for an ironic smile, hoping to imply I'd meant it as a joke.

Now Robin was towing a formidable-looking woman into the

office: the executive editor. "I've always admired your work"—
Alice Gochman embarked upon an obviously rehearsed speech—
"and I'm looking forward to improving the magazine. I'll work
very hard to help you revamp *Gourmet*."

I had to tell her the truth. "I'm sorry." I hoped I looked as
distressed as I was feeling. "I'm sure you're a very important part
of this magazine, but James Truman said I could bring in my own
people. I don't have many, but I do have someone I'm trying to
persuade to be my executive editor. I'd like you to stay; surely we
can find something for you in another capacity."

The woman's face shut down.

"I'm not sure Laurie Ochoa will come," I temporized, "but we
worked together for almost ten years at the *Los Angeles Times*, and
we're kind of joined at the hip. I'm hoping she and her husband
will move to New York. But there's a lot to do, and I'm sure we can
find a job that will suit you."

She was saying, "I'll have to think about that," when an assistant ran in, calling, "We have a serious problem with an adjacency!"

Caught off guard, I failed to control my face, and Alice immediately saw the truth. Her lips turned up in an involuntary
grin. "Excuse me." She rose gleefully from her chair. "I'll have to
go deal with that." She walked off, a little skip in her step, the assistant trailing behind. Soon, I thought, the entire staff will know
that the new editor in chief has never heard of an adjacency.

When the door closed behind them, I slumped across the desk,
burying my face in my hands. I'd only been here an hour and already I was out of my depth. *Gourmet* felt like an alternate universe
whose citizens spoke a language I did not understand. I needed a
translator.

I peeked out of my office, thinking Robin might be able to

help. But she was whispering into the phone. "And listen to this: She doesn't even have a secretary!"

Humiliated, I tiptoed back to the desk. It was a long time before I learned what Robin's words meant or understood how much I had revealed when I said I was on my own.

A personal secretary is not an assistant intent on moving up the ladder. A good secretary learns everything about the boss, becoming so essential that when the executive gets promoted, the secretary comes too. I had just admitted that I was a novice in this corporate world, and Robin was both relieved and elated. She would not only get to keep her job, but she could also show me the ropes. I know that now, but at the time I was convinced she was laughing at me, and I was determined to do something about it. Picking up the phone, I dialed the one person who would know the answers to all my questions. "What the hell," I asked Donna Warner, the editor in chief of *Metropolitan Home,* "is an adjacency?"

Donna and I had few secrets from each other. She'd started out as the food editor of *Apartment Life,* and in the early years, when I was freelancing for the magazine, we came to know each other well. Gentle and easygoing, she was constantly coming to my rescue. In the early eighties, when I wanted to go to New Orleans for the American Cuisine Symposium, Donna said, "I'll go too. Then you can save money and share my hotel room." We romped through New Orleans, eating and drinking like lunatics, and finally, desperate for vegetables, ended up sneaking away from the symposium in search of salad. I knew she would never betray me.

"Take me to dinner," she said now, "and I'll give you a crash course in magazines 101."

* * *

WE MET AT THE RESTAURANT I was currently reviewing, an ambitious place intent on introducing luxury health food to wealthy New Yorkers, and Donna got right down to business.

It wasn't rocket science, although Donna laughed so hard when I told her that an editor had said she was "a wizard with inadequate sep" that people all over the restaurant turned to stare at us.

"She was bragging; nobody's a wizard at sep. All advertisers want to go ahead of their competition, but there's no magical way to separate them. You just have to work it out."

"Does that have anything to do with the teeosee?"

Donna laughed again. "That's not a word," she said when she finally stopped. "It's initials: table of contents."

I felt like an idiot.

By the time Donna finished explaining the economics of the ad/edit ratio, we were on dessert and the "tea sommelier" was hovering over us, pontificating about "hints of smoke among notes of honey and sherry." When he finally wound down, Donna turned to me. "Have you met your managing editor?"

I tried to remember the people Robin had introduced. "I think there was this pretty young woman with dark hair who had that title. She kept telling me how creative she was."

"Then you're in trouble. Creativity is not in the job description. You need a bean counter, a taskmaster, someone to make the train run on time."

"Sounds awful."

Donna nodded. "Most MEs are pretty grim, but they're the bad guys, which means you don't have to be. Believe me, you want such a person. If *Gourmet*'s ME thinks creativity is part of the job, get someone new. And don't"—she held my eye, emphasizing the point—"hire someone you like. I know you; you hate conflict and you want everything to be nice."

As I said, Donna and I have known each other for a long time. When I sighed she said, "Trust me, if you hire someone you like, they're not going to be good at the job. And you're going to need someone good. People all over New York are saying that Si's done it again. He brings Tina Brown to *The New Yorker,* where she promptly loses millions. Now he's handing *Gourmet* over to a restaurant critic. A colleague called today and said he'd bet me anything you'd be gone in a year."

"Thanks for telling me that," I said.

"And I said," she continued, "that I'd bet him anything he cared to wager that he was wrong."

We left the restaurant early. Donna had a train to catch and I couldn't wait to go home and crawl into bed. I was glad Michael was out of town; I didn't want him to know how demoralized I was.

But Nick was still awake, and I was absurdly happy to see him. A better mother, I thought, would be worried about his losing sleep, but just the sight of him made all the other stuff seem small.

"I'm hungry," he said when the babysitter had gone.

"Didn't Anisa make dinner for you?"

"Yes. But it wasn't as good as the food you cook." My son has always known exactly how to play me.

"It's kind of late."

"Please." He looked up at me. "Please."

What the hell, I thought; end the day on a high note. "How about spicy noodles?" They could be ready in a flash.

Nick nodded, happily following me into the kitchen, bare feet slapping against the floor. He hoisted himself onto the counter and, as the scent of ginger, scallions, and black beans rose around us, regaled me with tales of his day.

I boiled the pasta and tossed it into the wok, swirling it with a flourish. As I ladled noodles into Nick's bowl, I inhaled the scent, thinking how much better this was than anything the restaurant had served us. I reached for another bowl, and we took them into the living room, sat down on the sofa, and slurped noodles together. "I'm really going to like it," he said, "when you're home every night to cook dinner."

SPICY CHINESE NOODLES

. . .

½ pound Chinese noodles, dried egg noodles, or spaghetti

Peanut oil

½-inch-long piece of fresh ginger

2 scallions

1 teaspoon sugar

2 tablespoons Chinese black bean paste with garlic

1 tablespoon Chinese bean paste with chili

½ pound ground pork

Sesame oil

Cook the noodles in boiling water until al dente (the time will vary with the type of noodle). Drain, toss with a half tablespoon of peanut oil, and set aside.

Peel and mince the ginger (you should have about two tablespoons).

Chop the white parts and slice the green parts of the scallions.

Mix the sugar and the two kinds of hot bean paste, and set aside.

Heat a wok until a drop of water skitters across the surface. Add a tablespoon of peanut oil, toss in the ginger, and stir-fry for about half a minute, until the fragrance is hovering over the wok.

Add the pork and white scallions and stir-fry until all traces of pink have disappeared. Add the bean sauce mixture and cook and stir for about 2 minutes.

Stir in the green scallions and noodles and quickly toss. Add a drop of sesame oil and turn into two small bowls. This makes a perfect snack for two.

8

THE YAFFY

OF ALL THE KITCHENS I'VE INHABITED, MY FAVORITE WAS THE HIGH-ceilinged Victorian room in Berkeley with its ancient stove. Bedraggled ferns dangled from macramé-covered pots, and Stella the cat was always perched atop the highest cupboard, purring loudly. We never knew how many people would show up for dinner, so we always cooked for a crowd; for ten years I fed at least a dozen people every night.

Everybody pitched in. Stella sat regally surveying the scene as we rolled pasta out by hand on an ancient chitarra, cured our own sausages, cleaned squid, and stretched a single chicken to feed us all.

We'd lovingly constructed that kitchen, board by board, sourcing every single item at the flea market: the industrial stainless-steel sink that stretched across an entire wall, the granite for one counter, and the butcher block for the other. We lived communally, so there was always someone sitting at the round table in the corner, nursing a cup of coffee or a glass of wine. I cannot remember a single moment, day or night, when the kitchen was empty.

I loved the light in that room, the way the sun bounced off the lemon-yellow walls, making the wood gleam. I loved the cozy feeling, the camaraderie, the music that was always playing, and the curved glass bowl sitting on top of the refrigerator, filled with eggs. (It was a Dale Chihuly reject, rescued from a glassblowing workshop where I'd once cooked.) The last thing I expected was to walk into *Gourmet*'s test kitchen and feel that it was much the same.

I'D HEARD A LOT ABOUT the magazine's kitchen over the years, and I'd always imagined a large, imposing room filled with gleaming stoves, modern equipment, and frighteningly scientific cooks armed with stopwatches and thermometers. But when I pushed open the door, I found that the room was smaller and far more modest than I'd anticipated. The four ordinary stoves looked a lot like the one in my apartment, and the jumble of counters and tables lent the room a slightly cluttered air. It was a home kitchen writ large: cozy, messy, and filled with delicious aromas. The cooks, all women, were chatting noisily, like neighbors who had gathered for a party. I wanted to pull up a chair and spend the day.

As I stood there drinking in the scene, a pale thin woman in a chef's coat suddenly shouted, "Taste!" Picking up forks, the cooks came running from every corner of the room, skidding to a halt before a nut-topped chocolate cake. It was, I thought, a little early in the morning to be eating sweets.

"Let me remind you all that it's just a yaffy." The thin woman said the word with obvious distaste, as she took the first bite. She swallowed and held out her hand. "I'm Kempy, deputy food editor." She turned to a slim, startlingly pretty blonde. "Don't you think the chocolate's weak?"

The blonde put out a protective hand, as if to shield the cake from criticism.

"Is Zanne here?" I asked.

Kempy, her attention focused on a short woman with a broad face who was frowning down at the cake, did not answer. The short woman worried the chocolate with her fork. "I think the crumb needs help," she pronounced.

"This," said Kempy, "is Lori. She's a very talented baker. And that"—she pointed to the blonde, who'd obviously made the cake—"is Amy. She's a wonderful baker too." Gesturing around the circle, Kempy introduced the six cooks, who were all studying the cake with extraordinary focus.

Amy seemed determined to defend her cake, but with each criticism she looked a little sadder. "I could try using better chocolate?" She was almost whispering the words. "And the frosting— it's nothing but mascarpone with a little sugar whisked in. I could play around with it."

"Mascarpone?" Kempy sounded alarmed. "We can't ask our readers to source an obscure ingredient for a yaffy. Did you try cream cheese?"

Amy shook her head, her thin body drooping in defeat. She seemed to take this very personally, shrinking back each time another cook stepped aggressively into the circle.

"I'd up the sugar." Lori was plying her fork again. "And maybe a touch of vanilla?"

"I like Amy's cake!" The voice was deep, and as he joined the group I thought how strange it was to see a man among this gaggle of cooks. I studied him: Solidly built, with a humorous, lived-in face, he was not wearing a chef's jacket. Then I spied the camera in his hand and it came back to me: Romulo, the photographer, was now in the room.

"Well, you would, wouldn't you?" The voice was venomous, the accent slightly foreign. Australian? As a stylish young woman with long red hair stepped forward, I noticed Romulo stiffen. Like him, she wore civilian clothes. Her fork swept forward to snatch a corner. She put it in her mouth, which twisted slightly in distaste. Still grimacing, she turned to me, holding out a hand.

"We haven't met. Felicity." Art director, I remembered. "We're lucky this cake is only a yaffy, because we won't have to shoot it."

"But it's so pretty," Amy interjected.

Felicity shook her head. "It wouldn't matter if it was the most beautiful cake on earth. . . ." She looked straight at the photographer and shook her head. He lifted his chin defiantly and stared right back.

An awkward silence descended on the room. Romulo shifted awkwardly from one foot to the other, and in the sudden quiet the sound of the three kitchen assistants busily loading dishwashers and scrubbing pots grew very loud.

Zanne Stewart chose that moment to make her entrance. An icon in the food world, she was a tall elegant woman who'd spent her entire career at *Gourmet,* working her way up from answering phones to running the test kitchen. Her stature, her impeccable taste, and her intimacy with everyone who counted in the food world—she knew Julia and Jacques and Marcella—were extremely intimidating. But I'd learned, over the years, that she had a hard-drinking past and an improbably bawdy sense of humor. Now I wondered what had made me think such a lively person could possibly preside over a sterile kitchen.

Zanne's helmet of hair swung across her face as she sheared off a slice of cake, the gesture so swift it sent the silver bangles on her wrist clanging. "We'll shoot something else. It's only a yaffy."

She turned to give me a quick hug. "Sorry I wasn't here for the big show yesterday, but Julia was in town. I didn't think you'd mind. She's pushing ninety, and who knows how many more chances I'm going to get? Oh, yes," she added, "I also have a message from Marcella. She really wants to meet with you. I think she and Victor want to write a column."

I'd met Marcella Hazan only once, at a book event. Her fans had walked in bearing armloads of books, eager for her to sign them. I absolutely understood; even now when I'm asked which cookbook I'd choose if I could have only one, it's always a Marcella classic. "I love your simple tomato sauce," I'd told her then. "It's my son's favorite dish."

But the moment the words were out of my mouth, I wished I could snatch them back—this was no way to impress her. Marcella's tomato sauce might be the world's easiest recipe: It has only three ingredients.

"The one with the *honion?*" she asked in her syrupy Italian accent.

"That one," I said, overwhelmed by such strong synesthesia that I could smell the tomatoes and butter slowly slumping into each other as they simmered into sauce. It is the most comforting aroma I know.

"I like it too." She gave my arm a generous pat.

Marcella is gone now, but each time I make that sauce she's there, just briefly, standing with me at the stove, patting my arm.

"Should we give them a column?" I asked Zanne.

"I'd be happy to get her recipes," she said. "But Victor has a reputation for being difficult. Why don't you meet with them and see what you think." She handed me a fork. "Have you tasted the yaffy?"

I took the fork cautiously, knowing that this was a test. I didn't want to say the wrong thing and give them the impression that I didn't know what I was doing. It was bad enough that the editors thought I was clueless.

I could feel their eyes upon me as I studied the jewel-like little cake, considering my options. I could begin by commenting on the praline topping: Was it too sweet, too bitter, perhaps too burnt? Maybe the pieces should be smaller? The chocolate was another obvious target; I'd suggest using one of higher quality. Should I speak up for the mascarpone?

Then the fork met my mouth, and my body was flooded with sensations as the dark, dense, near-bitterness of the cake collided with the crackling sweetness of the praline. The flavors tumbled about, a sensory circus that was finally tamed by the rich smoothness of the frosting. It was all I could do to keep from reaching for a second bite, extremely hard to hide my smile. I *knew* this cake.

The cooks' eyes bored into me. "I'm guessing"—I tried to sound tentative—"that this cake has an English pedigree."

"How did you *know*?" Amy's voice rose in surprise.

Zanne did a little double take.

"Unlike Americans, the English don't overdo the sugar in their chocolate cakes." The cooks gazed at me with obvious respect, and Zanne nodded sagely. "That praline's a nice touch; lovely texture. And I wouldn't mess with the mascarpone; cream cheese reads so carrot cake, don't you think?"

"But it's only a yaffy," objected Kempy.

I ignored the interruption. "And I do think you should try better chocolate. Maybe Scharffen Berger?"

"Scharffen Berger?" Again, Zanne looked impressed. The high-end chocolate was new to the market, and she had not expected me to know it. I was, after all, a critic, not a cook.

"It's excellent chocolate, and I find it really makes a difference in baking. And it seems to me that the cake might benefit from more eggs." I looked at Amy. "Give it more body and improve the crumb."

"Not a bad idea." All eyes swiveled to Amy. "The recipe only calls for one egg," she explained.

I turned toward the art director. "A couple more eggs would give it more height too. . . ." Her lips began to curve into a triumphant smile and I hastily added, "But I don't think it needs it. It's such a gem of a cake." The smile vanished.

"That was excellent." Zanne's eyes danced. "Thanks. I hope you'll be joining us for tastes. We'd love to have your input." She turned to address her troops. "Amy, you know the drill. Try it again with Scharffen Berger. I think you should do it with Ghirardelli and Guittard too. And try adding two more eggs."

"Zanne!" Kempy was obviously annoyed, and I tried to remember what Zanne had told me about her deputy. Was there some friction between them? The two had been working together for more than twenty years. "We're completely backed up, and it's just a yaffy."

"But it's the only chocolate recipe in the May issue." Zanne turned to explain to me. "The readers love chocolate. Our best-selling issue of all time had a chocolate cake on the cover."

"Let me shoot it." Romulo gave the art director a challenging look. "It's a very pretty cake and I could really romance it."

The redhead made a deprecating sound, deep in her throat. The photographer's fingers twitched, but he said nothing and his adversary started for the door. There was another awkward silence.

This, I thought, would be a good moment to step in. "Please," I said. "What's a yaffy?"

Zanne gave me a grateful smile. "You Asked For It. Y.A.F.I.

It's one of our most popular features, one that's been a *Gourmet* staple since the very beginning."

"But there's something about yaffys you don't like."

"You noticed! The truth is, chefs are terrible at paring their recipes down for home cooks. The ones they send us never work, and we end up having to do them again and again to get them right."

"Must get expensive," I said.

"That's one of the things I want to talk to you about." She eased me gently out the door. "Got a minute?"

Just outside was a table laden with food. "We put it out here so everyone can taste what we're working on," she explained. "It gives the editors a way of participating in the life of the kitchen."

"Nice touch," I said. "I love the way your kitchen feels. So open. And the cooks—"

Zanne interrupted me. "We call them food editors."

"Well, they're cooks to me, and that's a compliment. I don't think you can be a good cook unless you have a generous soul. But that tasting process seems brutal; do you go through it for all the recipes or just the yaffys?"

"All of them. We test our recipes until they can't possibly get better. Sometimes we'll test a recipe twenty times."

"Twenty times?" It struck me as obsessive to the point of insanity, but Zanne ignored my obvious shock. "How on earth," she asked, "did you know that the cake was English? And don't give me any more baloney about the English not overdoing sugar. For that matter, how did you guess the recipe was short on eggs?"

"My impeccable palate, of course."

She stopped and stared, regarding me with new respect. "You're really good! The food editors were blown away."

I was tempted, for just a moment, to let it lie. But nobody's palate is that good. "It was crazy luck," I admitted. "Last year when we were in London, Nick ordered chocolate cake in a little café—I think it was called Café Mezzo. He liked it so much I asked for the recipe."

"And you recognized it?"

"It's an unusual recipe, and I've made it a few times. It really does taste better with Scharffen Berger. As I said, I got lucky. . . ." We were walking again, but now I stopped her. "My turn to ask a question: What's going on between Romulo and the art director?"

She inhaled sharply. "The situation's poisonous. Romulo's been here for years. We all love him; he's really talented and he has the most wonderful sense of humor. He can mimic anyone—I can't wait to see what he'll do with you. But when our art director retired last year, Felicity came in and started giving all the plum jobs to other photographers. He's miserable." She stopped and then added, almost reluctantly, "And he's not the only one. You'll see."

This cake is very easy, but the crushed-praline topping gives it a jewel-like quality that is rather spectacular. It's hard to think of another dessert that offers so much for so little effort.

JEWELED CHOCOLATE CAKE

(Adapted from Café Mezzo)

• • •

⅓ cup cocoa powder, plus more for dusting pan (not Dutch process)

3 ounces good-quality bittersweet chocolate

6 tablespoons butter

⅓ cup neutral vegetable oil

⅔ cup water

1 cup sugar

2 eggs

1¼ cup all-purpose flour

2 teaspoons baking powder

½ teaspoon salt

⅓ cup buttermilk

Preheat the oven to 300 degrees.

Butter a deep 9-inch round cake pan and line the bottom with parchment paper. Butter the paper and dust it with cocoa powder.

Melt the chocolate with the cocoa, butter, oil, and water over low heat, stirring until smooth. Remove from the heat and whisk in the sugar.

Cool completely, then whisk in the eggs, one at a time.

Combine the flour, baking powder, and salt, and whisk into the chocolate mixture. Shake the buttermilk well, measure, and stir that in.

Pour the batter into the pan and bake on the middle shelf of the oven for about 45 minutes or until a toothpick comes out clean.

Cool on a rack for 10 minutes, then turn out, peel the parchment from the bottom, and allow to cool completely.

Praline

½ cup slivered blanched almonds

½ cup blanched hazelnuts

¼ cup water

¾ cup sugar

Toast the nuts in a 350-degree oven for 10 minutes. (If you're using hazelnuts with skins, put them in a towel and rub the skins off, but don't bother being fussy about it. Whatever comes off easily is fine.)

Combine the water and sugar in a small saucepan and bring to a boil, stirring until the sugar dissolves. Boil without stirring until it begins to darken, swirling the pan until the mixture turns a beautiful deep gold. It takes a while for the mixture to darken, but once it does it goes very quickly, so don't walk away or it will burn. Remove from the heat and stir in the nuts.

Pour onto a baking sheet that you've lined with foil, parchment, or a Silpat, spreading evenly. Use an oven mitt—a burn from hot sugar can be very painful. Allow to cool completely.

Break into pieces, put into a plastic bag, and smash with a rolling pin until you have lovely crushed pieces you can sprinkle over the frosting, adding both crunch and flavor.

Frosting

Mix 2 tablespoons of sugar into a cup of mascarpone. Spread the frosting on the cooled cake and heap the praline bits on top.

9

BITTER SALAD

I GLANCED AT MY WATCH AND MY HEART BEGAN TO RACE: LATE again. I had to pick Nick up in fifteen minutes.

"Gotta go," I shouted at Robin, running out the door and sprinting down the street to the subway. By the time I reached the school, panting and out of breath, only two forlorn children were still standing on the steps.

Nick's look of relief quickly changed, and his face clouded with accusation as he ran down to meet me. "Why can't you get here on time?"

"I'm sorry, sweetie." These days that's all I seemed to say. I bent to kiss him, inhaling the deliciously yeasty little-boy scent.

I'd known, almost instantly, that promising to be at *Gourmet* every day was a mistake. I just hadn't known how big, hadn't realized how frantic I would become trying to do two jobs.

And I'd forgotten all about the book tour.

"What an opportunity!" Maurie gushed when she learned

that the paperback edition of my first memoir, *Tender at the Bone,* was going to be published that spring. She took immediate charge. "This can be your unveiling. Do you know how much press we'll get? *Everyone* wants to know what you look like when you're not in disguise."

Maurie's formidable publicity machine ground into gear. Then it was joined by my book publisher's, and a perfect storm of media attention came raining down. Richard Avedon was on the phone, Ann Curry, Terry Gross, Susan Stamberg. Louisville offered me the keys to the city if only I'd show up. The *Today* show followed me around for a week.

At first it was exciting. Then it was just exhausting. I'd wake, already apprehensive, at four every morning and drag myself out of bed to write the scripts for my daily restaurant review on WQXR (the station was owned by *The New York Times*), thinking, hurry up, hurry up, hurry up. I'd be away for almost a month, which meant prerecording every show. I was eating out sixteen times a week, trying to get ahead of my restaurant schedule, and between meals, when I wasn't posing for the press, I was shuttling back and forth between the newspaper and the magazine. I was always frantic, always late. The few hours with Nick were the best part of every day, but I was making a mess of that too.

"I should never have said I'd be at the magazine while I was still at the paper," I'd said as Michael and I lay in bed, hoping for sleep. "And now there's this national book tour. . . ."

Michael heaved a deep sigh. "I have something to tell you. . . ." I braced myself. "You know that piece I pitched a couple months ago on nuclear terrorism? All of a sudden they want it right away. I'm leaving for Colorado in a couple of days and I'm not sure how long I'll be gone."

I went numb with fury. Now? He was leaving now?

"I know the timing's bad." Was that an apology? "Who's going to look after Nick while you're away?"

Rage had overwhelmed me: While *I* was away? What about him? The feeling was as familiar as a toothache. Things may be better now—although I have my doubts—but in 1999 when a child got sick at school, the nurse never called the father. Working men did what was convenient; working women did everything else. And felt constantly guilty: No matter where you were, it always felt like the wrong place.

Later, when young editors came to tell me they were pregnant but planned to keep working, I'd find myself warning them about the guilt to come. Because all the talk about "quality time" is utter nonsense; children don't need quality time. They need your time. Lots of it. And they let you know it.

When Nick was six, he made it very clear that he was not getting enough from his work-obsessed parents. "You need to spend more time with him," Michael said. And I agreed; it did not occur to either of us that *he* might be the one to change his schedule. As a restaurant critic, I had no way to spend my nights at home, but days were a different matter. So no more nanny: I was now the one who picked Nick up at school, standing on the sidewalk at 3 o'clock alongside a posse of hired caregivers.

The change in Nick's attitude toward me was dramatic. He had always been the sweetest child, but as he began to trust that I would be there every day, he stopped being on his best behavior. Now every bad thing that happened was my fault. And that was fine with me; I didn't want my son treating me with kid gloves. Children, I came to understand, need you around, even if they ignore you. In fact they need you around so they can ignore you.

"But how will I find the time?" the young editors always asked. It's a reasonable question; you have to give up something. We each find our own answers. In my case, I gave up sleep; after Nick was born I discovered I really didn't need that much, or at least that I could get by on just a few hours. To this day, I feel guilty spending more than five hours in bed, as if I'm being profligate with precious time that could be better spent. I also saw less of my friends. That is, until Nick was a talking, sentient being and they all wanted to be his adopted relatives.

Now, as Nick and I walked home from school, I realized the book tour would also have to go. We had no New York relatives, and I could not possibly leave town for a month. I tried figuring out how I'd break this to my publishers, who had spent months working on the tour schedule. They were not going to be pleased. I was so distracted that when we entered the apartment to find my brother there, it took a moment to register. My brother lives halfway around the world.

"What are you doing here?" I asked as Nick ran joyfully to greet him.

"You sounded desperate when we spoke last week," Bob said simply. "So I decided I should come help out."

I'm not a crier, but I was so overcome that I burst into tears, unable to believe this unexpected answer to my problems. "Can you spare a month?"

"My kids are grown. My marriage is a mess. And I have some time off. If you want to know the truth, I can't think of anything I'd rather do than spend a month in New York with Nick."

Bob has always been the perfect brother. Thirteen years older than me, he's the child of my mother's first marriage, and we've never really shared a house. He lived in Pittsburgh with his father when I was growing up. But he'd come home on holidays, arriving late to sneak me out for hot-fudge sundaes in the middle of the night. He came to visit when I was at camp, sometimes took me along on dates, and was always the first person I called when

Mom was at her craziest. Even when he was living abroad with a family of his own, he'd always been there when I needed him. But this time it had seemed too much to ask.

Bob's one of those extraordinarily gregarious people who make instant friends with strangers; after two days of school pick-ups he was intimate with mothers whose names I didn't even know. He organized games in the park, took kids out for pizza, made elaborate weekend plans. And he happily spent entire afternoons wandering the aisles of FAO Schwarz with my son. "Don't worry about us," Nick said importantly as I left for the airport. "Bob and I are going to be bachelors together."

I suspected that meant brownies on demand, no baths, TV at all hours. I didn't care. Nick was happy. As I stood waiting to board the airplane, it hit me that for the first time in months I did not feel guilty.

Then reality intruded. "Ruth!" The voice was familiar. "You going to L.A. too?"

It was Paul Goldberger and David Remnick. Paul had been culture editor when I arrived at the *Times,* which made him, briefly, my boss. With his pale skin, small nose, and soft mouth, he always made me think of an extremely dapper rabbit. He was, as usual, beautifully dressed, clutching the most elegant carry-on I'd ever seen. Glancing at the rope dividing us, he said incredulously, "Are you flying *coach?*"

"Book tour," I explained.

The two men exchanged glances. "But you're at Condé Nast now," said Paul. "You're an editor in chief."

"I'm not actually on the payroll." Why did I feel so defensive? "I don't start for almost two months."

"But you shouldn't be traveling like that."

It sounded like an accusation; I was supposed to be a member of their club, and I obviously didn't know the rules.

"Where are you staying?" His voice was hopeful.

My heart sank; no redemption here. "The Hilton," I mumbled.

"The Hilton . . ." Paul's voice went squeaky with distress. Once again the two men exchanged glances, and I could feel my face getting hotter. Even the hotel's location—the intersection of L.A.'s two noisiest thoroughfares—was undesirable.

At that moment the loudspeaker announced that the first-class passengers were about to board, and the men loped toward the plane with the unhurried assurance of privilege. I looked after them, clutching my battered suitcase. I had never traveled first class in my life.

I worried the entire flight that they would see the friends who were collecting me at the airport. It would do my Condé Nast cred no good to be caught climbing into a battered, rusted-out old pickup.

I need not have worried. By the time my carriage came wheezing and hiccupping to a stop, the Condé Nast limos were long gone. "Sorry we're late," said Laurie.

Some things don't change.

In the mid-eighties, when I became the restaurant critic of the *Los Angeles Times,* I kept running into the same young couple when I went out to eat. Did they, I wondered, spend all their time in restaurants? You couldn't miss them; they were extremely conspicuous in the small Asian and Mexican restaurants they seemed to favor.

He was pale and puffy with long, thinning hair and the mushroom complexion of someone who rarely sees the sun. She was tall, with golden skin, wild black hair, and a lean body that seemed to be all legs. No matter the weather he wore a scuffed black motorcycle jacket, while she favored bright prints in clashing colors. They were such an improbable pair that every eye invariably swiveled toward them.

For months we pointedly ignored each other. Then a waiter in some tiny Koreatown restaurant specializing in tofu insisted we share a table. We were the only non-Asian patrons in the place, and the man refused to take no for an answer.

Slowly, reluctantly, we began to talk. Jonathan Gold turned out to be the music critic of the city's alternative paper, *LA Weekly*, but there seemed to be no subject on which he lacked an opinion. The girlfriend, who also worked at *LA Weekly*, was as silent as he was voluble. Most of the time she sat watching him with large liquid eyes, nodding thoughtfully as he spoke.

He was a classical cellist and rap music aficionado who was close to people with names like Snoop Dogg and Dr. Dre. He also claimed to have eaten at every taco stand in the city. I found this hard to believe, but it turned out to be true. Jonathan also knew a stunning amount about Thai and Korean food and could go on for hours about the distinctions between the foods of Uzbekistan and Tajikistan. I found him slightly pompous, irritating, and utterly fascinating. I was pretty sure he felt the same way about me—minus the fascinating part.

Over the next year our edgy relationship did not prevent us from sharing many meals. Jonathan always talked a lot; his girlfriend rarely said much. So when Jonathan suggested I hire her as my assistant at the *L.A. Times*, I was disinclined.

"You should consider Laurie," he insisted. "She's the smartest person I know."

I doubted that.

"I know Laurie's quiet," he persisted, "but I promise you she's the best editor I've ever met. The least you could do is talk to her."

It was a long time before I realized how much this must have cost him. Jonathan was a competitive person who wanted to be the best at everything he did. And he already knew what I was about to find out: Laurie Ochoa is one of those self-effacing people with a genius for making others look good. Unambitious for herself, she is enormously supportive of those she loves. She's improved the work of every writer she's ever worked with, and I am certainly no exception.

She asked endlessly thoughtful questions about my articles, picking up each word, touching it, tasting it, willing it to be the perfect fit. She read things into my writing I hadn't known were there, so that each time I saw them in print I found myself thinking, did I really say that?

She was also extremely demanding. It was Laurie, in her quietly tenacious way, who insisted we try to take over the food section. "Think what we could do with all that space!" she kept saying as she urged me to write a proposal. I got all the credit for the excellence of the section, but at least half the ideas were Laurie's, and I could never have done it without her.

Now I wondered how I could persuade her to move to New York. She'd agreed to consider it, but she'd seemed unenthusiastic, and as Jonathan drove, gears shrieking, to a Sichuan restaurant in the San Gabriel Valley, I marshaled my arguments. I planned to broach the topic at the table, so it was disappointing to find a few of their more eclectic friends—an experimental novelist, an avant-garde composer, and a performance artist—already there. I'd have to wait to make my case.

The proprietors greeted Jonathan with reverence and immediately brought out a huge hot pot, a vast metal bowl filled with meat and vegetables. While the others stuck to the vegetables, Laurie and I happily fished out sliced pig intestines and cubes of congealed blood; among other things, we share a taste for strong flavors. "I wonder," said Jonathan as he watched us eat, "if there are any restaurants like this in New York?"

"We'll have plenty of time to investigate," Laurie replied.

And that is how I found out that they'd both decided to join the *Gourmet* experiment.

* * *

AIRPORTS. HOTELS. ROOM SERVICE. INTERVIEWS. In my memory, the book tour remains a blur of small-town America and endless plane rides. And then, at last, I was on my way back to New York and the final appearance on the schedule.

"Can Bob and I come with you?" asked Nick.

I looked at him, surprised. "You don't think you'll be bored? I'm just going to give a little talk and sign some books. It's not all that interesting."

"But I want to see what you've been doing while you were gone."

"There are never any kids there," I warned him.

I was wrong about that. At the end of the reading, the very first person in line was a man pushing his small son toward me. "You owe him an apology," he said.

Nick moved in closer to hear.

"I was the chef at Capsouto Frères," the man continued.

This was not going to be good.

" 'Bitter salad,' " he quoted sourly—he had memorized the entire review. " 'Mushy sole. Cottony bread.' They fired me after your hatchet job, and I haven't been able to find work since."

I sat there, chagrined and embarrassed as the man glared at me, unmoving, hand on his boy's shoulder. I did not know what to say.

My brother stepped smoothly into the silence. "This," Bob said, bringing up the next person in line, "is Evelyn. She says her mother was an even worse cook than ours. As if such a thing were possible." Still glaring at me, the chef moved on, pushing his son before him.

Shaken, I looked at Nick, wondering how he'd taken it. In

more than twenty years as a restaurant critic, I had never been confronted in public, and when anyone asked how I felt about negative reviews, my answer was cavalier. "You can't be a good critic," I'd say blithely, "unless you're willing to tell the truth. Nobody believes a critic who only says nice things."

But I wasn't being honest. I never wrote a negative review without worrying about closed restaurants, lost jobs, and fired chefs; there was no joy in thinking about the harm my words could cause.

"You can't be a restaurant critic," Mary Frances Fisher once told me, "unless you are one of those ambitious sorts, willing to walk on your grandmother's grave." I'd quoted that in the article about disapproving of what I did, the article that had sent Truman to see me. And then I'd refuted it, ending the article by quoting A. J. Liebling. "All it really takes to be a restaurant critic," I'd written, "is a good appetite."

But I hadn't fooled myself; I'd taken the easy way out, and I knew it. Now, as the chef and his son walked away from me, I felt nothing but relief that my reviewing days were behind me.

10

HUMAN RESOURCES

"YOU'RE NOT GOING TO LIKE THE MANAGING EDITOR I'VE HIRED," I warned Laurie before her first day at the office. "I took Donna's advice and picked someone who's a serious bean counter. He seems like a total pain in the ass, but Human Resources has assured me he's the best ME in the building."

What they'd actually said was that the editor of *Allure* was distraught to be losing Larry Karol. Since I'd pretty much hated him on sight, I had a hard time understanding why she was so upset; I thought I was doing her a favor.

He was a tall, thin stork of a man who stalked into my office, disapproval etched into every line of his body. His head was small, the hair so closely cropped that you couldn't help noticing his compact, neat ears. His face bore so few distinguishing characteristics I thought that if you tried to describe him you'd end up noting his impeccable posture and that he was very, very clean. When

I introduced Laurie, he studied her long hair and colorful clothing, making no attempt to hide his dismay.

"Not very corporate." Did he actually say the words? But it was easy to tell what he was thinking. He shook her hand and then turned on his heel. "I'm going to walk around and get the lay of the land," he called over his shoulder as he strode off. Laurie and I looked at each other, mouths twitching; he couldn't wait to escape.

An hour later he was back. "This place"—his voice was strangled—"is insane! It's not a magazine; it's like some girls' seminary from the last century. Their procedures are absolutely archaic; I can't imagine how such inefficiency has been permitted."

Larry had discovered, in less than an hour, something that had completely eluded me: The magazine had no support staff.

"You didn't notice that there were no copy editors?" Larry was incredulous. So was I. My copy editor at *The New York Times*, Don Caswell, had become my best friend and constant savior; was there no one at *Gourmet* who made sure the copy flowed smoothly and the grammar was correct?

"And," he continued, "the complete lack of fact-checkers escaped your attention?" I gulped; fact-checkers are the ultimate defense against errors. Didn't anybody question *Gourmet*'s writers on their sources? Was there nobody who made sure that what the magazine printed was actually true?

And Larry wasn't finished. "Are you telling me that you didn't know that *Gourmet* has no photo editor?"

"That's not possible!" I cried. "This is Condé Nast. There must be somebody on staff who figures out which photographers to use."

He shook his head. "There isn't. I guess the art director just calls her friends." His scathing look telegraphed, in a single second, how outraged he was, how hopeless I was, and his deep regret at having accepted the job. "I'm going to have to reorganize everything, from the bottom up." He gave me another searing look. "Do you have the faintest idea what you're doing?"

I shook my head miserably; there was no point in denying it.

"Did you notice," Laurie said when he'd stalked off again, "that beneath all that bluster he seemed rather pleased? He doesn't want us to know it, but he *likes* the idea of shaking everything up. It gives him a chance to create his own systems."

"I had no idea they were so short-staffed." The head of HR sounded genuinely chagrined when I called to say we'd need to hire a few people. "But why are you there?" Jill Bright did not try to hide her surprise. "You're not due to start for another month."

Back in January, when I accepted the job, I'd insisted on having some time off after leaving the paper. That, of course, was before I'd rashly promised the staff that I'd come to *Gourmet* every day. "Are things so bad," Jill asked, "that you felt you had to start early?"

That wasn't it, although there had been a certain pleasure in watching Larry question everyone on the most minute details of the magazine's workflow. Most of the time I had no idea what he was talking about, so I followed him around as he met with production people, paper experts, color correctors, and lab technicians. It was a crash course in the technical side of magazine-making.

At least twice a week Larry stormed into my office shaking his head over some new and even more outrageous situation he'd uncovered. Mostly I just listened. But when he came in holding out a budget report, his hands shaking with emotion, I sat up and took notice.

"Have you seen the production budget?" he raged. "It's tiny. *Vogue* spends more on a single photo shoot than *Gourmet* spends on an entire issue. I'm guessing the former editor tried to save money so she'd stay below the radar." He gave me a rare smile. "That worked out well for her, didn't it?"

Larry, I knew, was more than capable of reorganizing the magazine without any help from me.

I was also taking enormous pleasure in watching Laurie conduct her own reconnaissance, slowly getting acquainted with the staff. She was, in her quiet way, as irate as Larry. "What a waste of resources! There's so much talent here and it's been squandered. The former editorial team made all the decisions at the top. None of the other editors ever got to share their ideas. Do you know what one senior editor told me?"

She was so angry she had to stop to compose herself. "She said she had never made a single assignment of her own. The executive editor simply doled out the manuscripts, and when they were done editing she'd come in with a ruler, pull up a chair, and go over it."

"Oh, my God, it's like something out of Dickens."

"Exactly! And given the level of expertise in this staff . . . They're all so smart, they know so much about food, and they have so many interesting ideas!" She told me that Jane Lear was a walking food encyclopedia who could answer questions about arcane ingredients and techniques without having to look anything up.

"I know," I said. "A couple of weeks ago I asked her an innocent question about sesame seeds and she gave me an entire treatise on benne and how the seeds arrived from Africa with the slave trade. She even went into the science of the seeds."

"She is," said Laurie, "a national treasure. Do you know how lucky we are to have that kind of resource? Then there's Jocelyn Zuckerman, one of the younger editors, who's extraordinarily well read. She gave me a list of the writers she'd like to work with: Junot Díaz, Ann Beattie, Jane Smiley, David Foster Wallace . . .

And that's just for starters. She has a whole list of young literary writers I've never even heard of."

Laurie had learned that the lone male editor, James Rodewald, was passionate about wine and itching to make *Gourmet*'s wine coverage more appealing to younger oenophiles. "And I can't wait," she said, "for you to see the way Romulo imitates your walk. He had the entire kitchen laughing until they were crying."

Laurie didn't need me any more than Larry did, so it was certainly not a sense of duty that brought me in the door every day. As I struggled to explain why I'd started early, I tried to put my feelings into words. The energy in that office was so potent, it was as if we'd pulled the cork on a bottle of champagne and released a vibrant explosion. At the *Los Angeles Times*, Laurie and I had done all the heavy lifting; here we didn't have to do a thing. When we asked, "What do you think we ought to do?" the staff invented an entirely new magazine. They were bursting with ideas—for writers, for columns, for special issues—and it was exhilarating. Magazine-making is a collaborative process, and watching *Gourmet* grow and change was so enthralling that I didn't want to miss a single day.

When I'd contemplated the job I'd worried about the burden of being a boss, afraid the staff would fear and resent me. But now I saw that there was another side to that coin: Nothing feels as good as building a team and empowering people, watching them grow and thrive.

A Condé Nast honcho once carped that I was "too accessible." I considered that a great compliment. When I'd arrived a quiet haze of depression had been hanging over the office and it had now been replaced by animation, noise, constant conversation. People talked in the halls, gathered in the kitchen, so filled with ideas that the whole place felt as if it was humming.

Larry watched it all with an air of benign amusement. "It

might be a good thing," he conceded one day, "that you and Laurie are so new to this. You don't know what's not possible, so you just keep saying yes. It's a bit anarchic, but it certainly makes life interesting."

It would have killed me to admit it, but without Larry we'd have been lost. Nobody was thrilled with his new procedures—we were all marching to his tune—but each day the place ran a little more smoothly. We might resent his endless tinkering, but Larry made us all feel safe.

We were an odd trio, Laurie, Larry, and I, but we had perfect equilibrium, and before long we each began to understand our role in the institution we were creating. I was the cheerleader, the instigator, creating chaos, insisting we make changes right up to the last minute when someone came up with a better idea. The staid magazine, which had always operated at a stately pace, was now speeding along in a constant state of flux. Laurie was the nurturer, mopping up behind me, always calm, always available, always ready to talk. And Larry was the disciplinarian who kept us all in line.

But there was more to Larry than met the eye. He had an uncanny ability to see beneath the surface and an unerring instinct for talent. Over time he hired the most remarkable people.

"You sure about this?" I said when he introduced our new copy editor, a skinny Brit with bad teeth and a shaved head, dressed almost entirely in leather and enveloped in a cloud of invisible smoke. "He looks like the drummer in a punk band."

"That's exactly what he used to be," Larry replied. "Two bands, actually: One was called the Art Attacks. The other was the Monochrome Set."

"And you want him for a copy editor? Don't you think he's weird?"

Larry gave me his coolest stare. "And how, exactly," he said, "would that make him different from you?"

Despite his appearance, John Haney turned out to be curious, meticulous, detail-oriented, and extremely literary; he was, in short, the perfect copy editor and a vital part of the new *Gourmet* we were creating.

The huge chasm between the old and the new did not become entirely clear for a few more months. But in the fall, when we moved into our new offices, Zanne suggested I invite Jane Montant, who had edited the magazine in its halcyon years, to come to tea. "It would be a gracious gesture," she said. "Mrs. Montant would appreciate it. You should invite Ronny Jaques too; he was our photographer for many years. He lives in Europe, but he's in town for a few days, and you really ought to meet him."

Mrs. Montant swept into my office like a great yacht, towing the petite photographer in her wake. Even at eighty-three she was an elegant creature, with silver hair and a determined gait. She stopped stock-still in the center and stared critically around, making an obvious effort to hide her distaste for the brightly colored modern furniture.

White-haired and rosy-cheeked, Ronny was quite a contrast. Eyes twinkling, he gazed curiously at each object with the air of a friendly leprechaun, looking so young it was almost impossible to accept that he was nearly ninety. Ronny had worked for many magazines during a long and distinguished career, photographing everyone who mattered—royalty, stars, politicians. You instantly knew that this man was comfortable in his own skin.

"We had so much fun!" he cried as I poured them each a glass of wine. Tea, it seemed, held no interest for them.

"We did!" Mrs. M. turned to him. "Remember that day in Florence when the traffic was so terrible?"

"Of course." The sparkling eyes took on a wicked gleam. "The traffic just stopped."

"So"—she turned to me—"we got out of our rented car, left it in the middle of the street, and went to eat."

"You mean you just abandoned the car so it was blocking the street?" I was unable to keep the horrified fascination from my voice.

"Oh, yes." Her reply was regal, implying this was the only sensible way to deal with such irritating inconvenience. "The meal was wonderful. After a leisurely lunch we strolled back and picked up the car." She smiled benevolently. "The traffic was clear by then."

I tried to imagine any situation in which I might do such a thing. I could not. "In those days"—Mrs. M. seemed to be reading my mind—"we knew how to live." She gave me a condescending smile. Then, gaze shifting, she looked beyond me and her face changed as if she'd seen a ghost.

"What?" I asked.

"Mr. MacAusland," she said. "I was thinking about our founder; he was both editor and publisher, and he had a first-class temper, which he never bothered to control. One day, when our offices were still in the penthouse of the Plaza Hotel, he had such a ferocious argument with an editor that the guests on the floor below came upstairs to find out what all the noise was about."

"And what happened?"

"Oh." She waved a hand. "His secretary handled it beautifully. 'Think nothing of it,' she said. 'They're just rehearsing for the Christmas play.'"

I laughed, but it explained a lot. They had believed the whole world was their stage, and they strutted around as if they owned it. The *Gourmet* they'd created had reflected that particularly American sense of entitlement.

But we were very different people, living in a very different time. And the magazine we were trying to make was for our moment, not theirs. "We're having fun too," I said to Mrs. Montant, understanding for the first time how much I'd come to love this job.

11

THE DOWNSIDE

LUNCH WITH RALPH LAUREN. BREAKFAST WITH LEXUS. COCKTAILS with Chanel. Now that I'd left the *Times* and my job here was official, my publisher, Gina, seemed to have an endless parade of advertiser events requiring my attendance. I had no interest in any of this, but when I tried to refuse, she grew ice-cold.

She prepared me carefully for each meeting, and soon I understood that the magazine we were selling depended entirely on the needs of the client. *Gourmet* might be a lifestyle publication, a humble homemaker's bible, a travel magazine, or an epicurean pioneer. We might be upscale or strictly down-to-earth. On some days we emphasized the quality of our recipes; on others we acted as if they did not exist.

Gina herself was a chameleon, carefully dressing the part. Her clothes, her jewelry, and her watches changed with the impression she cared to convey. She never left a single detail to chance, and as I watched her operate I could not believe how wrong my first impression had been. There are many words to describe Gina Sanders; "ordinary" is not among them.

Bright, agile, and fast on her feet, she was the most competitive person I'd ever encountered. She never gave up, turned every lemon into lemonade, and obviously relished a fight. Conflict makes me so uncomfortable that I'll do almost anything to avoid it, but Gina got under my skin. There was something about her that made me fight back every time she put up her fists.

Our biggest battles were over the travel editor. I wanted someone younger, with a more modern outlook; Gina was extremely satisfied with the travel editor we had. Why wouldn't she be? Pat was a pleasant older woman, but she was neither a writer nor an editor and devoted most of her time to representing the magazine at travel conventions. When she wasn't traveling, a constant stream of people from national tourism boards paraded through her office. These people oversaw impressive advertising budgets, which meant that Pat was far more important to Gina than she was to me. "I don't see why *we* should be paying her," said Larry. "If Gina is so fond of her, she can put her on the advertising payroll."

"Why would I do that?" Gina asked frostily when I broached the subject. She watched every penny like a hawk and was extremely content with the current arrangement. But Pat ostensibly worked for me, and each time I said I would replace her, Gina reminded me how important travel advertising was to *Gourmet*'s bottom line.

Whenever I screwed up the courage to ignore Gina's wishes, I thought of her most memorable remark. Driving home from an ad call, she'd turned to me with the look of a cat who'd swallowed a canary, saying, "I think we just took that business away from *Bon App*, which is extremely satisfying. Just winning isn't enough; I don't feel good unless the other person loses."

The message came through loud and clear.

My methods were a little less blatant, but when I saw an opportunity, I took it. The first time we went to lunch with a client, Gina's limo was late. "We're due in fifteen minutes and my driver's stuck in traffic," she said, gazing anxiously up the street. "I *hate* not being on time."

"We could take the subway," I suggested.

It was a completely innocent remark. To me, the subway is more than a quick way to get from one place to another. It is New York in miniature, an intimate glimpse of the city. You rub shoulders with everyone who lives here, find out what they're reading, see what they're wearing, eavesdrop on their conversations. I love the music of many languages, the wide-eyed amazement of the tourists, the impatience of the seasoned rider each time the train comes to one of its mysterious between-station stops. Riding in a taxi gives you privacy, but why would you want to be insulated from all this?

Gina, clearly, did not see the subway in the same light, and her horrified reaction gave me an idea. I tugged at her arm, pulling her down the sidewalk. "Come on," I urged, "it's just a couple of stops." Casting a final, despairing glance up the street, Gina reluctantly followed me down the subway stairs.

The train came roaring into the station with a metallic squeal of wheels, and I enjoyed her discomfort as she edged nervously back on the platform. Boarding the train, she pulled her shoulders in, making her body as compact as possible. "I don't take the subway much," she said, as if admitting something I didn't know. Lowering herself into the seat next to mine, she sat ramrod straight, assiduously avoiding body contact. "The first time Steven took me out on a date we took the subway," she confided. If this was an attempt to minimize the difference between us, it definitely did not work. "My father," she added disingenuously, "was absolutely appalled."

I thought it was time to change the subject. "Tell me about this lunch," I said.

She relaxed as we entered more comfortable territory. "Beauty is central to our business plan, and Estée Lauder is an important client. All I want you to do is remind Mr. Lauder how powerful you were as the restaurant critic of *The New York Times*. I'll do the rest."

She exited the train with obvious relief, but as we walked into the restaurant I noticed her glance at her watch. "Mr. Lauder just arrived," the maître d' assured us, leading us to a table occupied by an elegant older man with papery skin. He half-rose to greet us, offering a steely smile. Beautifully dressed, he wore his wealth proudly, and I thought, briefly, how different he was from Si.

There were polite preliminaries and then Gina looked pointedly in my direction. "What should we order?" Taking my cue, I tried to recall which of the dishes was most esoteric.

"Cold lamb's quarters soup," I said, thinking how pleasant it was to be in a fancy restaurant and not have to take notes. "Nobody else is doing anything remotely like it."

"Lamb's quarters?" Lauder looked intrigued.

"The world's most delicious weed. Jean-Georges is working with a forager who brings him wild greens. This one is like spinach with a college education: bright green, slightly spicy, very intense. He serves it with a little hash of hazelnuts and crab to coax out all the flavors: First you taste the forest and then the sea."

Gina nodded, silently applauding my little show.

"But I can never resist Jean-Georges's foie gras; he poaches it in sweet wine until the texture is unlike anything you've ever experienced. So fragile, like eating clouds."

"Ah," he said, remembering. "You gave the restaurant four stars, didn't you?"

Gina looked pleased.

The food was as fine as I'd remembered, and I ate dreamily, savoring the sweetbreads with their hints of ginger and rumors of mango. Gina, I noticed, was pushing her food around the plate, merely pretending to eat. I noted that food was not her friend; she seemed relieved when she could finally put down her fork and swing into her pitch, rhapsodizing about the upscale lifestyle publication we represented, the one whose five million readers routinely dressed up to go out for lunches just like this. What better place for the Lauders to advertise their lipstick, their perfume, their mascara? I was impressed.

At the end of the meal, after a deep-crimson tartare of cherries and an apricot tart, the waiter appeared with a cart laden with more sweets. We selected ornate chocolates and colorful cookies, and then the waiter removed the top from a delicate glass canister and pulled out long ropes of homemade marshmallow. As he cut them apart with silver scissors, Gina moved in to deliver the coup de grâce. "Do you know," she asked, looking earnestly across the table, "why Cartier and Tiffany advertise in *Gourmet*?"

Mesmerized, I shook my head, rapt as the client.

"Because fine restaurants are the only places for which Americans still dress up. Where else are women going to wear their makeup and jewels? Restaurants aren't like movies and the theater—they don't take place in the dark. Every time we go out to eat, we are the star of our own show, and we want to look our best. You *have* to advertise in *Gourmet*!"

"I think that went well," she said as we exited through the restaurant's gold-and-glass doors. The errant limo had caught up, and we climbed into the backseat. "I have a feeling you and I are going to be a great team. We've been in a battle in the marketplace, and your time and commitment to getting our message out to the ad community is going to mean so much."

She's still selling, I thought, she can't help herself. Only now I've become the client.

"There are so many sales calls I want to take you on!" As the pitch continued, alarm bells exploded in my head. The lunch hadn't been horrible, but in my twenty years at newspapers I'd never met a single advertiser. Even as editor of the *Los Angeles Times* food section, which brought in thirty-five million dollars a year, I had never been asked to sit down with an advertiser. I'd expected magazines to respect the same strict firewall between advertising and editorial. Indeed, Truman had made it sound as if the magazine's business was not my problem. Was spending time with advertisers really part of my job?

As soon as we got back to the office, I went stomping upstairs and, eschewing introductory small talk, blurted out, "Do I have to go out on sales calls?"

Truman looked up from his desk. "Every publisher appreciates the chance to take his editor along." He is never, I thought, at a loss for an answer.

"You're being evasive." I was too upset to be tactful. "Just answer the question: Is it part of my job?"

"Well," he admitted, "when I was an editor I hated it. So I did it so badly that my publishers stopped taking me."

"Thanks!" I left his office with a happy heart; he'd told me exactly what I wanted to hear.

Truman's words stayed with me the entire time I was at *Gourmet*, but as the years went on I began to see them very differently. At first I thought of them in a wistful way, hating myself for not being more Truman-like. But I just didn't have it in me. Was it because I'm a woman, trained to be a good girl and play by the rules?

Truman had related that tale with a kind of glee. Why wouldn't he? He'd figured out how to manipulate the system. And so, although I behaved with the grudging grace of a bratty teenager, each time Gina called, I went.

But in later years, when I was throwing myself wholeheartedly into the chase for advertising dollars, I wished I'd followed Truman's example when I still had the chance. And at the end, when my primary job had become the endless quest for the money that might save the magazine, I looked back at those words with incredulity: They were proof positive of how enormously our entire world had shifted.

12

THE FLORIO POTATO

"STEVE FLORIO WANTS TO SEE YOU." ROBIN TELEGRAPHED ALARM at this call from the CEO. "Right away."

"Why?"

"I don't know."

"But you always know!"

She shook her head. "Not this time."

Could it be Gina? Had she asked the chief executive officer to have a word about the travel editor? I could find no other explanation for this command appearance.

"His secretary"—Robin was whispering now, as if this was a dark secret—"told me he was furious when Truman hired you without consulting him. He doesn't like it when decisions are made behind his back."

"But he was recuperating from a heart attack! Besides, why would he care? He's Gina's boss, not mine."

"Try telling him that." She made a sour face. "As far as he's concerned, he's the boss of everyone. And you better not keep him waiting."

Robin stood up; if her cubicle had contained a door, she would have been holding it open. Casting an eye across my outfit, she produced a little frown. "You do know you have to use up your entire clothing allowance before the end of every year?"

This did not exactly lend me confidence.

I was still trying to acclimate to the opulence of my new office at 4 Times Square. Even larger than it had looked on paper, the airy, open space stretched up Broadway for much of the block between 42nd and 43rd Street. The honey-colored table gleamed, the carpet was thick and soft, the chairs were comfortably uphol-stered. The floor-to-ceiling windows looked down at the tourists scurrying across Times Square, making me feel like a princess in a tower. Compared to Florio's, however, mine was a hovel. I found him ensconced in an enormous leather chair, his expressive face framed by a view stretching across Manhattan to the Hudson River and New Jersey beyond. Both the office and the man radi-ated confidence and money, and as the scent of expensive after-shave wafted toward me, I had a quick vision of the roly-poly banker on the get-out-of-jail-free card in Monopoly.

"I'm sorry we haven't had a chance to talk before." His face was tan, his cuff links gold, his shave so smooth around the big mustache I would have bet a barber showed up daily. "You know, you're very fortunate to have Gina as your publisher."

So that *was* why I was here.

"You know she's in the family?"

I nodded, silently beginning to sweat.

"Did she tell you they gather for family dinner every Sun-day?"

Where was this going? "She did tell me that." In a rare moment of candor, Gina had groused about the Newhouse *New Yorker* ritual. Advance copies of the magazine were delivered on Sunday morning, and to her disgust you had to arrive at dinner prepared to discuss every detail. The meal, as she described it, sounded like the exam from hell.

"The man's impossible!" Steve boomed. I jumped, startled. "Calls me at all hours of the day and night. There I was, in the hospital, barely alive, tubes everywhere, and he's calling to discuss ad pages. . . ."

For the next fifteen minutes Florio regaled me with tales of life with Si, growing more loquacious by the minute. "You know that Roy Cohn was his closest friend?" I shook my head, unable to imagine Si hobnobbing with America's fiercest red-baiter. "Roy, of course, was a closeted homosexual."

Florio let that hang in the air as he moved on to Si's children ("He's so mean to them"), and his elegant wife, Victoria ("Did you know her first husband was a count?").

I kept waiting for him to get to the point, tell me my job was in jeopardy unless I began kowtowing to my publisher. Instead, he complimented me on my clothing ("You look just like a little China doll") and asked about my office ("I must come see what you've done with it!").

Overwhelmed by his oratory, I let the words pour over me. I'd never met anyone remotely like this large, loud man, and I didn't understand why I found him so appealing. He was launching into Victoria's fervent dedication to the Catholic faith ("So why did she marry a Jew?") when his words came screeching to a halt. I turned, seeking the reason, to find Truman striding toward us. Refusing a chair, he stationed himself at the window, just behind Florio.

Florio smoothly switched gears and began talking about food. "I am an extremely talented cook!" he announced, bursting into an epic recitation of a recent visit to a three-star Napa Valley restaurant. "Here's this fabulous place run by a world-famous chef, and the guy doesn't know the first thing about making Bolognese! So"—he demonstrated—"I rolled up my sleeves and showed him how to do it."

"Really?" He was a fabulous raconteur; I could almost smell the pork, the milk, the slowly caramelizing tomatoes.

"Yes!" Florio nodded his head vigorously, smiling with unabashed delight as he savored his own brilliance. Behind him, Truman was vigorously shaking his head in the opposite direction. I watched this pantomime, amazed. I stifled the urge to laugh: Steve remained utterly oblivious.

"Not one word of that was true!" Truman said as he walked me down the long corporate hall to the elevator. Florio, in person, had been so completely convincing that I'd forgotten the *Fortune* magazine reporter who had caught him brazenly lying about everything from the company's numbers (wildly exaggerated) to his military record (nonexistent). Still, I gaped at Truman, shocked by his candor.

"Steve is the world's biggest liar." He said it with vehemence. I can't imagine much love was lost on the other side either: It is impossible to imagine two characters with less in common.

I turned, looking back down the corridor. Right in the corner, where it veered left, was Si's office. It was flanked by Florio's on the right, Truman's on the left, a little Bermuda Triangle of animosity. I wondered what had compelled Si to set himself squarely in the middle of an editorial director and chief executive officer who didn't get along. He was famous for the long hours he spent at the office, so he must enjoy it. But what did he get out of this ongoing acrimony?

"I'm assuming Steve called you up here," Truman was saying. "Why? What did he want?"

I punched the elevator button. "I don't have the faintest idea. All he did was talk."

"That," he said emphatically, "is one thing he's very good at."

"WHAT DID HE WANT?" LAURIE asked the minute I returned.

I repeated what I'd told Truman. "It was bizarre." I described how Truman had stood behind Florio's chair, shaking his head over the lies. "I don't think those two men have a single thing in common. Steve's a big, brash swaggerer who enjoys spending money. I think he's so accustomed to lying he doesn't even know he's doing it. Meanwhile, Truman's so self-contained. . . . He told me he spends a month every year at a silent retreat in some Buddhist monastery. I can't understand why Si would want to spend most of his waking hours with two men who can't stand each other."

"Some people are fueled by conflict," she said matter-of-factly. "But it's lucky for us that he can tolerate such different personalities. It's kind of amazing the way he doesn't interfere, just sets everything in play and watches what happens. Do you think anyone else would hand you a magazine and let you do what you want with it?"

Laurie had a point. Truman offered suggestions and Si occasionally questioned a cover, but neither had ever demanded that we make a change.

"I suppose," I said, "he believes in letting people make their own mistakes."

"Yeah. And when they make too many he gets rid of them. Don't forget that. You've never been very good at managing up, but this time you should cultivate a few friends in high places."

"Florio invited me to lunch at the Four Seasons."

"You have to go!"

To be honest, I was looking forward to it. I could not understand how I could like such a corporate creature, but for some reason I'd found Florio extremely endearing.

WALKING INTO THE FOUR SEASONS, I couldn't help thinking of my mother. For months before the restaurant opened in 1959, Mom pounced on every single word written about the luxurious new establishment. "It's called the Four Seasons because it's going to change with each season," she informed Dad and me. "Not just the menu, but the *entire décor* will be redone every three months!" She regaled us with breathless descriptions of the interior, designed by Mies van der Rohe and Philip Johnson, describing in minute detail the dramatic Richard Lippold sculpture hanging above the bar. "It's supposed to look like bronze icicles," she said. But what intrigued her most was the famous Picasso curtain.

"Think of it like a museum," she said the first time we went, leading us into the bar as if we were entering the Promised Land. I couldn't help noticing that inside this luxe landscape, Mom became a different person; she even seemed to breathe more happily in here.

While Mom and Dad nibbled nuts and nursed martinis, I enjoyed the city's most expensive glass of orange juice. But a single drink, no matter how slowly you sip, can last only so long. Mom sighed when Dad asked for the check, looking wistfully around: She longed to stay for dinner.

Still, the restaurant's spell stayed with Mom as we dined on fifty-cent sausages down the street at Zum Zum. Grateful for her continued happiness, Dad picked up her hand, wiped away a spot of mustard, and kissed it. "Someday," he promised, "I'll take you to dinner at the Four Seasons."

Sadly, he never did. Now, entering a room that still radiated power, I tried seeing it through my mother's eyes. It was not, I realized, a dining room: It was a kind of living theater.

I surveyed the captains of industry seated with such easy arrogance at their capacious tables: None of them had come to eat. They were here because they could be seen but never overheard. They were here because the light in the room made everyone look better. They were here to bask in the obsequious sarcasm of the owner, Julian Niccolini, an elegantly attired Tuscan with saturnine good looks, who made sure that meals for these extremely busy people never lasted too long. They were here because no annoying check was ever presented; when lunch was over they simply strolled off. (How Mom would have loved that little detail!) They were here, ultimately, because everybody else in their world was here too.

But Steve Florio was different. He was also here to eat.

"Have you experienced the Florio potato?" he asked as Julian led us to a prominent banquette in the center of the room.

Julian answered for me. "She has not."

"Then," said Florio regally, "we'll have two."

A few minutes later a pair of giant baked potatoes made their way across the vast dining room, each one modestly perched upon a plate, emitting little puffs of steam. As they got closer I could see that each had been slit open and paved, from one tip of its brown top to the other, with a wide, glistening swath of beluga caviar.

"Dig in," said Steve, sticking his fork into the middle of his spud. "They make these just for me." He glanced around the room to see if anyone was watching and noted, with some satisfaction, that he had captured the attention of the former mayor, seated at the next banquette. As his mouth closed over a mound of fish roe, he actually smacked his lips. "Fantastic!" he cried, a little too loudly. Philip Johnson, seated on the other side of us, turned to look.

Florio ordered a stunningly expensive Italian red wine to ac-
company the caviar and proceeded to regale me with sensational
tales of Si. Most were scurrilous and many untrue, but I nodded,
pretending to believe the myths about Si's scintillating private life.

The business stories were easier to swallow. Steve began by
bragging about all the money he'd lost during his tenure at *The
New Yorker.* "Si didn't mind," he said airily. "There have been
times when Condé Nast couldn't meet payroll and he simply wrote
a check." He leaned conspiratorially toward me, his forehead almost touching mine. "After I moved up, my brother Tom became
the publisher of *The New Yorker* for a while; we used to argue about
which of us had bigger losses."

"You boasted about *losing* Si's money?" I was incredulous.
"Didn't he mind?"

He waved a hand, batting the thought away. "Si doesn't mind
about the money; he just wants to be the best. But don't think you
can cross him; he really hates to lose. Has anyone told you about
the time one of the fashion books published a negative article
about a major Italian label?"

I shook my head.

"The designer retaliated by pulling his ads from every Condé
Nast publication." Steve picked up his glass, gave it a swirl, and
took an appreciative sip of the Gaja Barolo. "Si was furious. It was
the editor's fault, but Si punished the publisher. He made him fly
to Milan and undo the damage. Told him not to return unless he
succeeded."

"Doesn't seem fair," I said.

"Fair?" He laughed. "Si has no boundaries when it comes to
business. Has Gina told you about her father's funeral?"

"No."

He gave me a wicked grin. "During the service Si berated her
about lost ad pages."

"He didn't!"

"He did." Florio took another sip of the deep-red wine. "But don't worry—that will never happen to you. He behaves very differently toward the editorial side. He gives you all a lot of rope." He frowned resentfully down into his glass, then looked up, adding cheerily, "And then he lets you hang yourselves."

I looked at the salt-and-pepper hair, the big mustache, and he suddenly reminded me of Groucho Marx at his most sardonic. I wondered what had happened to the editor of the fashion magazine.

"Dessert?" he asked. I shook my head, but from across the room Julian was approaching with an extravagant cloud of fluff. Setting it before us, he leaned in to whisper, "Cotton candy gives our guests their childhood back. It's the only thing they don't have." Then he went gliding off to the next table.

Florio took a huge handful of spun sugar and stuffed it into his mouth. "What Julian doesn't understand," he said, "is that this is so much better than my childhood."

13

BIG FISH

WHEN I TOLD TRUMAN I NEEDED A NEW ART DIRECTOR, HE WAS unsurprised. "You've done twelve fine issues," he told me, "but your covers have been weak and your newsstand sales are terrible."

He didn't need to tell me that I was being judged on newsstand numbers; sales reports arrived on my desk at the start of every week, and I spent a great deal of time trying to make our covers appealing.

The problem was that, each time, Felicity would nod sagely and then totally misinterpret every word I'd said. I showed her a W. Eugene Smith photograph I loved, of a peasant woman standing in a field, wearing a radiant smile as she offers her cupped hands to the camera; you can't see what she's holding, but I've always imagined it's a mushroom of some kind. To me it captures all the generosity of cooks; it's as if she's saying, "Look at the treasure I've pulled out of the earth just for you." What Felicity shot was a skinny young model in a pink cashmere sweater, holding out a handful of berries. And so it went, month after month. I didn't like the covers, but more to the point, the readers didn't either.

I probably could have put up with that, had Felicity not made so many enemies at the magazine. Her feud with Romulo made everybody so miserable that I finally asked her to try being more tactful.

"I didn't come here to make friends," she snapped. And that was it for me: I wanted a happy workplace.

"I've been thinking," Truman said now, "that you and Diana LaGuardia might be well matched. She's been at the *Traveler* for a while, and she's getting restless. I think you'd like each other. Shall I arrange an introduction?"

Change, at Condé Nast, does not dawdle. The next morning I met Diana for breakfast. I had no trouble spotting her as she crossed the Algonquin dining room; the stylish middle-aged woman might have had ART DIRECTOR tattooed across her forehead. Her pale, clever face was bare of makeup, her dark hair was streaked with gray, and she was dressed entirely in black. Her short skirt revealed excellent legs and feet encased in hip lace-up oxfords; in a time when most women teetered about on very high heels, hers was a definite fashion statement.

"Is your father the book designer?" she asked, and immediately began talking type. Of course I liked her. She ordered a big breakfast—potatoes, eggs, and sausages—leaning into her food with unembarrassed appetite. I liked that too.

"WHAT PERFECT TIMING," SAID GINA when I introduced our new art director. "Our annual sales conference starts tomorrow. The reps are coming from all across the country, and they'll want to meet you."

I watched the two women circle each other, almost sniffing the air with suspicion. Gina, carefully coiffed and conservatively dressed in an understated suit, was cool and slightly aloof; she stood as far away as possible as she proffered her small hand. When Diana grabbed it, I wondered how my publisher would react. Diana didn't just shake your hand: An alpha dog, she sent a message.

Gina calmly reclaimed her hand, her face revealing nothing. "You could kick off our sales meeting," she said with a touch of hauteur, "by explaining your design philosophy to the staff."

Gina's annual meetings were legendary; it was the one thing on which she spared no expense. My first year she was hugely pregnant, but that did not prevent her from renting a fleet of motorcycles and roaring down Fifth Avenue on an enormous Harley. Another year she hired a voice coach, disguised herself as the Iron Lady, and addressed her staff in a perfect imitation of Margaret Thatcher. Once she floated in, scantily clad as Madonna, and sang "Material Girl."

But this year Gina outdid herself. She'd chosen *Enter the Dragon* as her theme. Shamelessly appropriating a cultural trope, she arrived at the office dressed in Chinese silks, her face painted chalk white and her head covered in a stiffly lacquered black wig, leading a troupe of entertainers carrying an enormous paper dragon. Banging drums, they went cavorting through 4 Times Square, bestowing luck.

But Diana was the one who roared.

"Let me"—she climbed onto the podium of Condé Nast's cozy corporate theater, shook back her hair, and straightened her short black skirt—"explain what I do." Diana was not tall, but she projected a distinct air of authority. "Our biggest problem is that advertisers are like cockroaches. We no sooner create a design than they colonize it, appropriating it in an attempt to make their ads look like editorial. So we have to keep changing what we do. It's my job to stay one step ahead of them."

A gasp ran through the room. The reps all looked appalled and I turned to Gina; even beneath the makeup I could see that her face had gone pale. "Please tell me she didn't just call the advertisers cockroaches!"

"She did!" I laughed, delighted by Diana's boldness. Gina shot me a glare of pure loathing. It was one more proof that I had taken Truman's words to heart and erected a firewall between advertising and editorial. One more proof that as far as I was concerned the magazine's economic health was not my problem.

But Diana, like most art directors, considered advertisers her mortal enemies. They were, she was convinced, intent on destroying the beauty of her work. She was always looking for new ways to get the better of them.

Never one to mince words, Diana stalked the halls of Condé Nast with the confidence of a creature who knows she's in her natural habitat. On her first day she marched into my office and tossed the current issue on my desk. "We can definitely do better." She opened the magazine and turned to "Gourmet Every Day," the section of quick, simple recipes we'd invented to overcome critiques of our recipes as too complicated. "You've been working backward."

"What do you mean?"

She pointed to the stiff rectangular photographs and long lines of text. "The copy is dictating the visuals. That's fine in the front of the book. But the well belongs to the art, and you should be working the other way around."

She'd lost me.

"Come. Let me show you." I followed her into the art department, where she stood at the light box, gesturing at layouts, talking with her hands. She gave off the clean, slightly medicinal scent of nicotine gum, which had a strangely sensual quality. "We're going to fit the recipes right into the photographs."

"I don't understand."

"If we get finished recipes from the cooks *before* we start shooting, we'll know exactly how much space the type will take up. Then Romulo can set up the photograph so the recipe literally becomes part of the picture. See? It will fit right inside. We'll waste less space and end up with a more dynamic page."

I was still lost, so Diana forged ahead. She and Romulo—thrilled that his nemesis was gone—began collaborating, and when Diana showed me the final result, I was stunned. The images were now married to the words, giving the pages a loose rhythm that invited you to cook. "What do you think?"

I looked at the picture she was holding: orange cream meringues splashed with a chocolate sauce that dripped so deliciously down the page I reached out a finger, thinking to take a taste. "I love it!"

Diana grinned and ran her hand across the image. I thought of my father: She was caressing the page as if the magazine were whispering secrets through her fingers, secrets she alone could hear. Even the little smile she wore resembled his. "Why hasn't anyone done this before?" I asked.

Diana shrugged. "I've never worked at a food book." It wasn't arrogance; she simply loved her work. Her redesign was clean and simple: The pages didn't draw attention to themselves, but each time I looked at them I heard my father's voice. "I want all traces of my work to vanish," he once told me, explaining that he was most successful when you did not notice the design. "All I want people to feel," he'd said, "is that they'll keep turning the pages because they're so easy to read.

"Now, book jackets," he'd continued, "are a different matter. They're supposed to catch your eye and keep it. Like magazine covers, they're mostly advertising. And that," he admitted rue-fully, "has never been my strong suit."

I worried that Diana was the same: better at the quiet interior than the loud, eye-catching cover. As the months passed I worried even more. Magazines make the bulk of their money in the fourth quarter, and I stressed about those end-of-the-year issues. Diana had encouraged Romulo to create a beautiful still life for the September produce issue, and its quiet beauty had performed well on the newsstand, but for October we needed something bolder. "Do you have any ideas for the restaurant issue?" I asked. "Last year's cover was a disaster."

That was putting it mildly. Laurie had dubbed Felicity's effort "Hitler youth at dinner," and the public obviously concurred: The issue racked up the worst newsstand sales figures in *Gourmet*'s history. "This year we need sales to be really strong."

"I do have an idea." I couldn't read the expression on Diana's face, but it looked a lot like mischief. "I want to find a really hand-some chef and get him to hold a giant fish. The bigger the better."

"We could ask Rocco DiSpirito," I mused. "He's handsome and talented—and kind of vain about the weight he's just lost. Do you think he'd do it?"

Diana stared at me. "Are you crazy? There's not a chef in America who wouldn't jump at this chance."

She was right about Rocco. Casting the fish, however, proved more difficult. It couldn't be any old cold-blooded creature with fins; this one required an impeccable pedigree. It had to be beau-tiful. It also had to be unendangered, unimported, and sustain-able. Not to mention very, very large.

Diana finally found her fish, a sleek creature nearly six feet long. Elegant as a model, the tilefish had lovely pale skin, clear eyes, and an extremely sassy tail.

But Diana fretted over the pose; how should Rocco hold his

piscine friend? In the end she had him dance with the fish, making it look more like his partner than something he planned to put on your plate. The image was romantic. It made you look. Then it made you laugh. And then it made you look again.

"I wonder what Truman will say?" As Diana handed me the neatly framed photograph, I detected a strange note in her voice.

When I handed Truman the picture, he took one look and dropped it so quickly it was as if it had burned his fingers. I looked down at the chef with the fish as Truman began backing away. "No, no, no," he moaned. He had turned slightly green. "Every magazine editor knows you can't put a dead fish on the cover."

Every art director must know it too.

"It's the first rule of magazines. Dead fish are a curse. The issue will never sell."

"But it's such a beautiful fish."

"You can't put a dead fish on the cover!" As he stubbornly repeated the phrase, I began to understand what Diana was up to: She was testing my mettle.

"I'll make you a bet." Diana had given me new confidence, and I was not about to let her down. I looked into Truman's unhappy face. "One hundred dollars says this cover sells more than last year."

He returned my stare. He looked down at the cover. "Last year, you might remember, was a newsstand disaster."

"The year before, then."

He looked at the cover one more time, studying it with great care. "You're on," he said at last.

That left Si. To my distress, I had to be out of town when it was time to present the upcoming issue to the bigwigs in the building. That meant Laurie had the unenviable task of introducing the boss to the fish. "You have to call me," I said, "the minute the meeting's over. I want to know exactly what happens."

"Si was dozing," she reported, "but when I showed them the cover he sat bolt upright and said, 'You can't put a fish on the cover.'"

"And what did you say?"

"I said, 'Ruth likes it.' And I just kept repeating that. Over and over. They all hated the cover, but nobody demanded that we change it.

"I kept invoking your name," she continued, "and I thought we were home free." I wondered if I would have had the strength to withstand that kind of pressure. "I turned to leave, and just as I reached the door Si said, 'Come with me.'"

"Oh, no!" Such a thing had never happened to me.

"He led me into Truman's office," she continued, "and threw the cover on the desk. Truman looked up and Si said exactly five words. 'Have you considered this carefully?'"

"What did Truman say?"

" 'Yes.' "

"That's all?"

"That was it. It was really fascinating, like they have this un-spoken means of communication."

"Then what happened?"

"Si picked up the cover, handed it to me, and nodded once."

"Oh, God." I was horrified. I had not realized I was putting Truman on the line. "This issue better sell. A lot."

I worried about that cover for the entire month, and once it was printed I haunted the newsstands. The piles seemed to be going down, but I couldn't be sure. The night before the first newsstand report, I was so nervous I couldn't sleep, and the next morning I got to the office early.

Truman had beaten me there.

Sitting on my desk were five crisp twenty-dollar bills. There was also a note. "Si and I have been talking; we think you should forget about turkey this year. Just put a fish on your November cover."

I picked up the bills and stood staring down at them, thinking how different this was from the last time I'd gambled on a fish.

A few years earlier, still at the *Times,* I'd submitted three fish-centric reviews to the James Beard Foundation for the restaurant criticism award. I didn't have much hope—Alan Richman, *GQ's* critic, always won—so it was a thrill to learn that I was, at last, a finalist. I could not, of course, blow my anonymity by attending an event filled with chefs, so the editor of the dining section, Rick Flaste, went in my place.

In those days the Beards were not nearly as flashy as they have since become, and in that pre-social-media era, there was no outlet to report the winners. Rick said nothing, so I figured Alan had once again taken home the trophy and I forgot all about it. I was, therefore, astonished a few days later when I got a congratulatory note from the Beard Foundation.

"Why didn't you tell me I'd won?" I asked Rick.

"Didn't I?" he replied carelessly. "I guess I forgot."

And that, I thought, was the difference between the *Times* and Condé Nast. To the *Times* I was just a food writer who didn't really count. Despite my prominent position there, I'd never felt like more than a cog in a vast machine, someone who could be easily replaced. It was different at Condé Nast; they took what I was doing seriously. To me, those twenty-dollar bills represented more than money: They were proof positive that Truman had my back.

14

BIRTHDAY

"THIS IS VERY GOOD," ROBIN BREATHED AS SHE HANDED ME THE thickly embossed invitation. "The only other editors invited to Si's birthday are AnnaGraydonDavidPaige." She ran the names of Condé Nast's most important editors together, seeming to consider my elevation into this exalted group a point of personal pride. "The invitation says no gifts, but what are you going to wear?"

I couldn't imagine.

"Anna will be there," Robin persisted. I thought of the last time I'd shared a room with the supreme fashionista; she'd been dressed in a silky teal dress trimmed with pale puffs of gray fur that looked so soft I wanted to reach out and pet them. On her feet were tall butter-colored suede boots that would surely dissolve with the first drop of rain. I pictured myself, the dowdy in a room filled with fabulously gowned women swanning through Si's legendary art collection, as turbaned waiters proffered extravagant tidbits and bartenders set spectacular cocktails on fire. Even the pre-party—Si celebrated each year by remastering a vintage film for a private screening at the Museum of Modern Art—sounded exotic.

"You *have* to get a driver." Robin stood by my desk, hands on hips, face screwed into her fiercest frown. "If you don't, you'll be the only editor on the bus." This, her stance implied, would be deeply humiliating to her.

"The bus?"

"Si hires a bus to take the other guests from the museum to his house. But the editors all take their own drivers. You *can't* get on the bus."

I was not about to be one-upped by AnnaGraydonDavidPaige. On the night of the party, I let her call a car. "Ask for Mustafa when you get downstairs," she said.

The man standing by the sleek black Mercedes was short and thick, with a rugged pockmarked face. As he held the door I noticed he had the hands of a boxer: calloused, large, strong.

"You don't use cars." The sentence, uttered in a heavy Arabic accent, was an accusation.

"How do you know?"

He slid behind the wheel and looked into the rearview mirror with a sardonic lift of the eyebrow. "When a new editor comes to Condé Nast, everyone is hopeful. Maybe we can be their regular driver." I liked the deep, gravelly sound of his voice. "But you? You make us all sad. You never use a car. You don't bring us a penny."

He glanced into the mirror again, smiling to indicate this was a joke. But I could feel the disapproval leaking through the humor. "The subway's so much quicker." My voice was small; why did I feel the need to apologize?

"But there's a line in your budget for car service! Why waste it?"

"Tell me where you're from."

He took the hint. "Egypt." Turning the wheel, he slipped smoothly into the line of cars heading north. "Alexandria. My city is so beautiful."

WALKING DOWN THE RAMP OF the museum's intimate theater, I looked around, disappointed. There was not a gown in sight, and I was glad I'd opted for the vintage couture cocktail suit, the last remnant of Chloe, one of the most successful disguises from my restaurant critic days. It was black satin, tightly fitted, elegant but not over the top; it was also the most expensive garment I owned. The other guests, dressed mostly in drab business suits, were grouped in uncomfortable clusters with vast spaces between the rows. They whispered uneasily to one another, trying to look busy as they avoided eye contact. I was grateful that Michael was already there, and he leapt from his seat, waving energetically. I slid in next to him, making little shushing motions with my hand as I looked around. None of the editors Robin had mentioned seemed to be in attendance.

We sat in edgy silence until Andrew Sarris, the *Village Voice*'s venerable movie critic, lurched onto the stage to offer an erudite little lecture about the movie we were about to see. He was a large, gnarled man who resembled an ancient hobbit, and there was a smattering of embarrassed applause. The lights went down.

I was enthralled by the romantic old French gangster film, but I couldn't help noticing the people all around me tapping surreptitiously on their BlackBerrys as it played. Latecomers snuck in, filling the back rows. The air prickled with impatience, and when the lights came up a palpable sense of relief flooded the room. As we stood, I noticed that the editors Robin had mentioned, all chic and important-looking, now occupied the back row.

A large bus waited outside, and as I watched the guests climb on, I saw that Robin was right: No editors were among them. On cue a phalanx of limos rounded the corner, purring out of the mist.

I peered at the identical sedans. "How will we know which one is ours?" Michael asked.

"That one." I pointed at the thickset man, sturdy as a fireplug, leaping from the first car. "Meet Mustafa. He's from Egypt."

My husband stuck out his hand. "Michael," he said, and began peppering the man with questions about Middle East politics. By the time the car pulled up to the huge glass monolith on the East River, they were so deep in conversation that Michael made no move to get out. "You go." He pointed upward. "This is so much more interesting than anything that's going to happen up there."

"Mr. Mike." Mustafa gave him a look of deep reproach. "You cannot abandon Miss Ruth. You don't know what it's like at the party. What if she needs some backup?"

He had a friend for life.

The lobby—majestic and dramatically dark—was filled with minions waiting to relieve us of our coats. They ushered us into the elevator and we ascended in heavy silence. The doors sprang open at the top to reveal a blindingly white vista, and we exited en masse to march down a wide hallway lined on both sides with vintage movie posters.

The door at the end was open, revealing a huge art-filled space hanging over the river. Even from the hallway I recognized a Picasso, a Giacometti, a Hirst. Curious about Si's life, I peered around, seeking signs of human habitation. But with the exception of some sofas and a few small round tables scattered through the rooms, this might have been a museum.

Many guests had apparently bypassed the entertainment portion of the evening; the apartment was already full of interesting-looking people clad in extravagantly different styles. Some wore drab business suits, some turtlenecks and jeans, but one woman passed me wearing a diamond tiara pinned into upswept hair, looking slightly ridiculous in this crowd. My vintage black cocktail suit also felt like overreaching, and I now wished I hadn't worn it. Chagrined, I knelt to examine the Damien Hirst cow, who stared balefully out from her formaldehyde-filled cube, as if wondering what she was doing there. "I feel the same, pal," I muttered.

"Did you say something, madam?" A waiter stood above me, holding a tray of glasses containing champagne and white wine.

"May I have some red wine?" I stood up, ducking to avoid his tray. The waiter gave me a look so disapproving that I took an involuntary step back.

"White wine only," he intoned in a sepulchral voice. His reproachful hand made a stately gesture, indicating the pale carpet, pale walls, pale sofa. He pointed to the art and thrust the tray of glasses aggressively in my direction.

Chastened, I took a glass. Michael followed suit.

Clutching the bubbly, we strolled the perimeter, feeling uncomfortable and out of place. "Just pretend we're in a museum," I whispered to Michael. "If only there was someone we knew, someone we could talk to." At that moment I spied Gina across the room and made my way toward her, thrilled by the sight of a familiar face.

My relationship with Gina was vastly improved, thanks to the travel editor. In a move that took us all by surprise, Pat had abruptly quit to care for an ailing husband. Before leaving, however, she had offered up the name of her handpicked successor, and Gina and I girded for battle.

"Never!" I told Larry when he suggested I interview the man. "I don't want another Pat."

"Just *see* the guy," he urged. "You don't have to hire him, but it would be a courtesy to Gina."

I'd learned by then that Larry was always right. And it would cost me very little. But the last thing I expected was the man who came bursting into my office, crying, "Couldn't I just bribe you to hire me?"

William Sertl threw himself into one of my red velvet chairs, radiating fellowship and energy. Large and rumpled, with a humorous face dominated by a long ski jump of a nose, he leaned forward and confided, "I've always wanted to work at *Gourmet*." Shooting me a roguish look, he added, "If you want to know the truth, I'm pretty sure Pat suggested me because she knows I'd do a terrible job. And," he added guilelessly, "if you respected what she was doing, that would be true."

Larry refused to be charmed. "I know you liked him," he said afterward, "but that man is not what we need." I watched him consider his next words, but he was never one to pull his punches. "He's too much like you and Laurie. How many free spirits can we have around here before the whole place falls apart?"

In the end, however, Larry conceded that hiring Sertl might be a good political move. "Gina will be grateful if you hire Pat's candidate. And if he disappoints her, she can't blame you."

It did not take long before we all realized that we'd lucked into the perfect person for the job. In addition to being a seasoned travel expert and a wonderful editor, Sertl had a million contacts and was an extremely entertaining writer. He roamed *Gourmet*'s halls with the irresistible curiosity of a child, poking his long anteater nose into everybody's business. This would have been annoying had he not been so effortlessly amusing; when you wanted to find Bill, all you had to do was listen for the laughter.

Once he strolled into a meeting saying, "Sorry I'm late. I was on the phone with Ann Patchett, who's deep in the Amazon. She just found a turtle at some jungle marketplace and couldn't bear to have it become somebody's dinner. She wanted to know if she could expense it."

"What'd you tell her?" Larry asked.

Sertl gave him his most innocent look. "I informed her of *Gourmet*'s policy, of course, the one that permits writers to expense any animal that rhymes with the name of their editor."

We erupted in mirth and spent the rest of the meeting figuring out what other animals *Gourmet* might be obliged to purchase.

Gina proved no more immune to Sertl's charm than the rest of us, and with the quarrel behind us, our partnership began edging into friendship.

"I'm so glad to see you," Gina said now, lifting a glass of water from a passing tray. "I've been dying to tell you about the strange encounter I had over the weekend. You're going to love this!"

She took a sip. "I ran into one of the old *Gourmet* editors at an afternoon tea." She mentioned a name; it was one of the patrician white-glove women who had chosen to leave when I arrived.

"Do people still have teas?"

"Old *Gourmet* people do." A little gurgle escaped. "She said she'd just come from a bar mitzvah. Then she made this funny little face and whispered, 'The kid's name is *Spencer* Shapiro. Don't you just hate it when they take our names?'"

My shout of laughter was such an unexpected sound in that hushed atmosphere that heads turned in our direction. David Remnick waved and strolled gracefully across the room. "Tell me what's funny."

More people drifted in our direction, and suddenly we were surrounded by an animated group of writers, artists, and politicians. Michael launched into a polite political argument with one of the *New Yorker* writers, and listening to them I was struck by a thought: if only Mom could be here.

"What I dream of," my mother wrote in her teenage diary, "is a life filled with culture and interesting people." As a young woman she'd moved from Cleveland to New York, chasing a life that turned out to be smaller than her dreams. Being in this room, I knew, would have made her very happy, and now I tried to see it from her perspective.

Michael was still deep in conversation, but I moved off, weaving through the crowd, shamelessly eavesdropping on the people I passed. "I thought about Brooklyn for the next home of Condé Nast," Si was saying to a small wiry guy in a skinny black suit, "but after you talked me into buying that sculpture by one of your Brooklyn artists, I changed my mind. It just didn't hold up. I don't think Brooklyn is the neighborhood for us."

Spotting me, Si came my way. Many eyes followed him, jealously looking to see whom he was favoring with attention. "I'm very pleased you're planning a major cookbook," he pronounced. "*Gourmet* hasn't done one for fifty years, and it is certainly time."

"It is." Unable to help myself, I added, "And I hope you're pleased with the advance." I wanted to make sure Si was aware that we were getting a million dollars; no Condé Nast book had ever earned that much.

"I am, of course, anticipating a major bestseller."

I glanced at his face, wondering if it was a joke. It wasn't. A million was good, he was implying, but he hoped that it was just the start, that royalties would come rolling in.

Annoyed, I bent down to commune with the cow. "Did you hear that?"

"Please tell me you aren't actually talking to that animal!" I didn't recognize the voice, but looking up I recognized the art dealer, he of the Brooklyn artist.

"I am indeed." I stood up. "I figure any cow who could find his way into this apartment might be able to talk. At least this cow didn't come from Brooklyn!"

He grinned. "The embarrassing mistake must be hidden away back there." He indicated a firmly shut door next to the entrance. At that moment the door swung open and two tiny pugs came scampering out, barking madly. In the instant before Victoria shooed them inside, we had a tantalizing glimpse of the private apartments beyond. Then the door closed.

"Did you know," the man asked, "that Si actually packed up his townhouse and moved into this apartment because of those creatures? Nero got too old to climb the stairs, so they moved in here. Had to give up most of his collection—more windows than walls—but he thought Nero would appreciate the view. He even built a ramp so the dog could see out better!"

I stored this delicious little morsel away; I hadn't heard it before. Si, like so many Americans, apparently found dogs easier to love than people.

"Every year," the dealer continued, "I hang around the door to Si's private apartments, hoping to find out what's hidden back there. I think it might tell me something about the private lives of the rich and famous."

"So you're not?"

"Rich and famous? Hardly. I occasionally sell Si a piece of art, but, you know, it's only Brooklyn, and that's not why I'm invited to this party. Si knows I share his passion for old movies, and I think he likes knowing there are other people in the theater enjoying *Pépé le Moko* as much as he is."

"Don't tell my secretary," I replied. "She's convinced this invitation is a mark of high favor, but I'm pretty sure I'm here for the same reason. I love old movies."

"We aren't the only ones." My new friend steered me through the room, pointing out a famous film writer, a director, MOMA's curator of films. "Mary Lea is great fun. Let's see if we can get her to join us for dinner. I promise you it won't be dull."

"Are we going to eat dinner together?"

"Of course we are! I will tell you scandalous gossip about the guests, and in return you will help me navigate the buffet table." A waiter passed, and he deftly scooped up the remaining caviar canapés. "Have a few." He slid some my way. "I always fill up on these. And I advise you to do the same."

As he steered me to the line forming in the next room, he whispered, "The wait for the buffet is always long, and when you finally reach the food, it isn't worth it. I'm hoping you'll have some advice for me."

"Rolls and butter." I filled my plate with carbohydrates. The bland country-club fare seemed to have been designed primarily to avoid staining the carpet; with the exception of overcooked salmon, it was all white. There was, of course, no garlic. "And save your appetite for dessert."

"Do you have inside information?"

"Yes. But don't get your hopes too high." Victoria had asked me to recommend a baker, but when I suggested a cake artist capable of creating something truly spectacular, Victoria demurred. What she wanted was red velvet.

The dealer's face fell. "Sweet chocolate fluff topped with sticky goo?"

"This will be a good version," I promised.

Later, as he rose to fetch a third slice, he turned to Michael. "This," he said, "is the finest dish ever served at this event. I know your wife thinks Si hired her to run a magazine. *He* might even think that. But as far as the rest of us are concerned, she's come to improve his birthday party."

"No," I replied, and it was as if Mom were there, speaking through me, "that's not true. At this party, the food could not matter less."

"GOOD PARTY?" MUSTAFA ASKED AS he drove us home.

"Interesting, actually," Michael conceded. "Although I'm pretty sure I would have had a better time talking to you."

But I was riding in a limousine, *my* limousine, watching buildings glide past in the cool autumn night, wishing my mother were alive. This was the city she had longed to inhabit, and she would have loved knowing I had breached its walls.

I would never really belong, but I'd been there for a year and a half, and the pieces were finally falling into place. The early angry letters from longtime subscribers—how dare we make changes to their beloved magazine?—had stopped and we were finding a new young audience. "I can't believe it," one venerable book agent had recently told me, "but my authors are asking if I can get them into *Gourmet!*" That felt like a triumph. But what most thrilled me was that our meetings had become raucous, and even the most timid of the editors were daring to speak up; the office felt like a happy place. As for me, for the first time in my life I was doing something that would have pleased Mom, made her proud. And for the first time in my life, I liked that.

"Mustafa." I inhaled and took a giant step into this new world. "Can you pick me up tomorrow and drive me to work?" I was just a visitor, a temporary passenger on the Condé Nast Express, but I might as well enjoy the ride every once in a while.

In the mirror, Mustafa grinned, grateful I'd gotten his message. "It will be my pleasure."

15

SEVERINE

DOM PÉRIGNON IS NOT THE IDEAL WAY TO GREET A NEW COUNTRY when you've been flying all night.

I know that.

Still, when the driver who picks me up at Charles de Gaulle takes me straight to lunch at Pierre Gagnaire, I do not refuse the crystal flute the waiter hands me. I watch the bubbles drift lazily to the top, inhale that fine aroma—grapes, yeast, and age—and take a sip. Pow! The champagne zooms straight to my head.

A crimson sorbet arrives cradled in a small glass dish. I dip in a spoon and a tumble of tomatoes, herbs, and horseradish, terrible in its cold tartness, assaults my mouth. The sorbet buzzes against my tongue, shocking me into the moment. One more bite, and I am experiencing the food with psychedelic intensity.

A tiny onion tart, no bigger than a fingernail, is crowned with a single bright nasturtium; I stare at the blossom, thinking this the most beautiful food I have ever encountered. Airy puffs of pastry enfold bits of fish and slices of caramelized apples that crunch and crackle merrily inside my head. Adorable shrimp dumplings nestle into leaves of lettuce, the sweet pink meat peeking shyly from each jade wrapper. The flavor is delicate, tender, and so seductive I want to keep it in my mouth forever.

But then I lift my glass and take a sip of cool white burgundy; the Corton-Charlemagne is so pure I imagine water trickling down a mountainside. I take another sip, and then another, of this gorgeous, heady wine.

Gagnaire's tribute to surf and turf arrives: delicate black caviar, pressed into a thick, fruity saline jam paired with foie gras that's been transformed into a trembling, almost liquid substance. I close my eyes and feel the flavors somersaulting through my mouth, a circus of sensations.

This is not my first major Paris meal. But it is my first as a civilian, the first time in my life I've dined in a three-star restaurant without standing back to appraise, consider, the first time I take not a single note. For once it is pure pleasure, and I find the experience intoxicating.

Lacquered duck skin with shiitake. *Lièvre à la royale,* the most decadent hare, served in three courses. And finally a cascade of desserts ending with a single prune stuffed with licorice root in a bitter sauce of caramel and quince. The insane flavors linger in my mouth, a tantalizing welcome to Paris.

Outside in the sweetly scented autumn air, the chauffeur is waiting. I climb into my car, dizzy with the meal, and float into my room.

But this is no room; the palatial suite at Le Meurice is filled with flowers, and down below the Tuileries spread out, glowing in the dusky late-afternoon light. "My own private garden," I think, and it is such a Marie Antoinette moment that I laugh out loud when I spy the cake on a little footed dish, the champagne cooling in its silver urn.

The bathroom is voluptuous, with its marble bath. Water gushes into the tub, and I toss in the perfumed salts and climb into water slick as glycerine. Leaning back, I savor the warmth, the space, the luxury. Then, wrapped in fluffy towels, I glide onto a bed that is like a huge soft cloud and go drifting off.

I was surprised when Larry signed off on the special Paris issue. "Paris sells," he'd said, "and I predict that this one will sell extremely well." (He was, as usual, right: The bestselling issue in *Gourmet*'s history, Paris sold out so completely that months later people were still calling, begging for copies.) Through some arcane accounting magic, Larry found the money to send most of the editorial staff to Paris. "It will be good for morale," he said, "and it won't cost significantly more than paying freelancers."

We travel in true Condé Nast style, staying at the city's finest hotels (although in the name of research we change hotels every night), testing the beds, the bathrooms, the service. Sertl forces us all to be guests from hell, dreaming up wicked tasks for the concierges. How quickly can they get a blouse cleaned, arrange a car, send flowers to an ailing friend? The cooks rent a giant apartment on the Île Saint-Louis with a kitchen overlooking the Seine and spend their days in markets, their nights replicating our favorite restaurant dishes. We work hard, but the sheer luxury makes us all slightly giddy.

This is a face of Paris I have never seen. Limousines chauffeur us from one three-star restaurant to another, and at night we meet for drinks at the Ritz. Money is no object; anything is possible. We start the day at L'Huîtrier, where we down oysters by the dozen, and then head to Barthélémy to munch our way through mountains of exquisite cheese.

On a manic shopping spree at the great kitchenware emporium E.Dehillerin, we load up on copper pots, Silpat molds (still unknown in the States), and jacquard kitchen towels by the dozens. I interview young chefs, get drunk with winemakers, and spend an entire afternoon at the Louvre, genuflecting before the paintings of Chardin. No artist ever had a more romantic relationship with food—or with his native city. The artist loved Paris so intensely he refused to set foot outside its gates, and on my last day I stand alone before his paintings, knowing exactly how he felt.

Afterward, I wander through crooked streets until I find myself in front of an elegant vintage clothing shop called La Petite Robe Noire. The place looks so forbiddingly chic that I hesitate to enter. Inside, a woman, her black hair cut into a Louise Brooks bob, caresses a small white dog. She looks up, catches my eye, and waves me imperiously in.

"I have the perfect dress for you." She lifts a cloud of black lace from a hanger. "It is a wonder. It is from Saint Laurent's second collection for Dior in 1959."

Cradling the armful of froth, she leads me to a corner of the shop roped off in black velvet and waits as I remove my clothes. As she slowly lowers the dress over my head, I notice a label sewn inside: "Severine."

"What does that mean?"

She produces a very Gallic shrug. "Who can say? Perhaps it is the name of the woman who owned the dress." She tugs the bodice, patting it gently like a beloved pet. "Don't look!" she commands.

As she meticulously closes each tiny hook, the dress enfolds me, until it is hugging my body like a lover. On her knees now, she finishes closing the dozens of hooks; this odd ritual seems to go on and on. At last she stands, tugging at the skirt, fluffing it a bit.

"This dress was meant for you. It is perfect." She leads me into the light and turns me, very slowly, to face the mirror.

I have been transformed. The woman in the glass is voluptuous, with curves in places I have never had them. A *dress* can do this? This person is glamorous. Elegant. She is Maria Callas. Paloma Picasso. Severine.

"You'll take it, of course." It is not a question.

I have never wanted anything so much as to be the woman in the mirror. Of course I'll take it. "How much does it cost?"

She waves a hand as if this is of no moment. "Let me negotiate with the proprietor of the shop." She goes to the desk, picks up the phone. "I assure you," she says in French, "this dress was meant for her!"

There is a silence. At last she gives an ecstatic cry. *"Merci, Didier, merci, merci."* Turning to me, she says, "He has agreed to take two thousand francs off the price! Your dress is only fifty thousand francs."

I nod, too dazed to do the calculation. And then I comprehend what she has said. "Sixty-five *hundred* dollars?"

For one wild moment I actually consider how I might pull off such an acquisition. But it is, of course, absurd. The woman is so disappointed that she takes her time releasing me, clearly hoping I will glance into the mirror and change my mind. The minutes crawl silently by. Finally her fingers separate the last hook from its eye, and I can step out of this amazing and impossible dress. I attempt an apology: "This dress belongs in a museum."

"Oh, no!" She gathers the dress to her bosom as if trying to console it. "Clothes were meant to be worn. And this dress was meant to be worn by *you*! You must reconsider." She presses her card into my hand. "You will"—she looks deeply in my eyes— "forever regret it if you leave Paris without this dress. Think about it."

I can't stop thinking about the dress. And then I can't stop thinking about the fact that I am thinking about it. If I don't buy the dress, I give up the woman I was in the mirror. If I do buy it,

I become a woman who spends thousands of dollars on a dress. There is no middle ground.

Suddenly I know exactly what I need to do.

THE NIGHT IS DAMP, THE streets misty and dreamlike. Rain has dappled the sidewalk with puddles that capture the lights of Paris in beautiful blurs of color. Nobody else is out, and I walk among the ancient buildings in a profound and satisfying silence until I reach the entrance of a small emporium.

I was seventeen the first time I came to Paris by myself. I rented a room in an austere pension near the Gare de Lyon run by the world's most suspicious landlady. Cabbage boiled endlessly in her small kitchen, and the sour smell pervaded the halls. I spent my days wandering the fancy food shops of Paris, gazing wistfully into Fauchon, Maison de la Truffe, Ladurée, and Androuet. But it was Caviar Kaspia that captured my imagination, and I began to save my francs.

At lunch I limited myself to bread and cheese. Nights I dined at a student cafeteria. When I had enough for a meal at Caviar Kaspia, I put on my one good dress and climbed the stairs to the small restaurant above the shop. Standing nervously on the threshold, I dared myself to enter. Then Yves Saint Laurent strolled past me, surrounded by an entourage of impossibly chic and beautiful people, and my confidence evaporated. I turned and fled.

Now I climb the stairs again, peering into the ageless restaurant with its wooden paneling, its fussy furniture, its tables swathed in cloth the color of sea foam. But when the maître d' greets me, I smile and follow him to a banquette near the window, where I watch the moon rise over the Madeleine across the way. I order lobster bisque, and as the aroma swirls around me I can almost feel myself leaping into turquoise waters, imagine diaphanous anemones waving their translucent arms . . .

"*Vous êtes seul?*"

How long has the old gentleman at the next table been trying to attract my attention? His skin is porcelain white, his hair silver and just a little too long, his eyes pale blue. He has a long, disdainful nose contradicted by full, sensual lips. A good face. And, I notice, elegant, slightly threadbare clothes whose patina of age makes them distinguished rather than shabby.

"Yes."

"You eat with such intensity! It has given me much pleasure to watch. You come to remember, yes?"

His speech is the stiff formal French of the past, when well-born people did not employ the casual *tu*, even within the family.

"Remember?"

He edges toward me on the banquette and inclines his head, a courtly gesture. "I have been coming here since before the war. That was a time when sturgeon filled the Caspian Sea, caviar was cheap, and Russian émigrés came to lament their lost dachas."

"I wish I had seen it then!"

"The room has not changed; only the clientele. *Merci, François.*" The waiter is removing a warm flute from the table; the new one he sets before my neighbor is silvered with cool mist. "*Un autre verre pour Madame.*"

The champagne is deep with the scent of honeyed almonds, the bubbles so lazy they barely make it to the surface.

He smiles. "An excellent vintage, this Krug '66. My father put down many cases; he said it was the perfect wine for caviar. But wait . . ." He scoops a great mound of glistening black roe from the bowl before him and hands me the plate.

"*Il faut respecter le beluga.* Eat it slowly. Hold it in your mouth for a moment before swallowing. The taste will change with the temperature."

The shock of freshness. The tang of the sea. And then the primal richness of the roe. A phrase of Lawrence Durrell's floats into my mind: "A taste as old as cold water."

He is watching me. "My wife ate caviar as you do. Slowly. Avidly. You put me in mind of her." He takes my plate, scoops on more caviar.

"What was she like?"

He sits back on the banquette and steeples his hands. "She was a mysterious creature. We were married more than fifty years, but I was never sure I knew what she was thinking. Never."

"Did you mind?"

He looks at me gravely, speaking slowly. "Not at all; it gave life flavor. Sometimes I look at this new generation, their casual ways, their easy familiarity, and I think how much they are missing. When I saw you sitting here, alone, I thought you were like a guest to yourself. And then I thought of my wife."

I try picturing his wife, but no image comes. "What was she called?"

"Severine."

The name reverberates through my whole body. Suddenly I am back in the shop and the dress is embracing me, turning me into someone I have never been.

My new friend motions for more champagne. The waiter arrives bearing two frosted glasses and we watch, wordlessly, as he fills them. Then my neighbor lifts his. "Thank you, my dear. For me this was a fortunate encounter. I did not know what brought me here tonight, but now I see that I wanted to try, just for a moment, to become the person I used to be."

"Fortunate for me too, Monsieur. For you have made me, just for the moment, into the person I might have been."

I reach into my purse, remove the woman's card, and tear it into pieces. I do not need her little black dress; it has already given me everything it can.

16

WHY WE COOK

THE OFFICES I PASSED WERE EMPTY. STRANGE, I THOUGHT, GLANC-
ing at my watch. Then I heard the babble of voices emerging from
the conference room and entered to find the entire staff staring,
rapt, at the television. I looked at the screen: The second plane
was flying into New York's tallest building.

"Ooooh," we said together, as if we had physically felt the im-
pact. After a moment of shocked silence someone said, "What do
we do now?" and every eye turned toward the door.

I turned too, wondering who was behind me. There was only
empty air. I froze. On the television, flames were leaping from the
burning building, which now had a hole in the middle. As the
implication sank in, panic surged through the room. We were
being attacked.

Think! I told myself, unsure what to do. I took two steps into
the hall, about to call upstairs and ask for instruction. The phones!
My head cleared; I went back into the conference room. "The

phone lines are going to be jammed, if they aren't already, so try to reach your kids and your families right now." They stared at me, not moving.

"Go!" I said. "Now! Make a meeting place. Public transportation may not be working, so factor that in. If this is really an attack, the police will close the bridges and tunnels, so those of you who live outside of Manhattan may not be able to get home. Come to my office; we need to be sure everyone has a safe place to go."

Nick! His school was in the Bronx. I turned to Robin. "Call Michael. Tell him he has to go get Nick before they close the bridges. Tell him to go quickly."

"I'd bet anything"—her voice held terrible assurance—"that he's already gone."

SHE WAS RIGHT, OF COURSE. While most people were still thinking this a freak accident, Michael's newsman's instinct propelled him out of the city. On the road before the second plane hit, he was the first parent to reach Nick's school.

"It's pandemonium." He was on the phone, begging me to leave the office. Behind him I could hear a small boy wailing that his father worked in the Twin Towers. "Why doesn't he call me?" he asked, hysterical, over and over. I heard Michael pick the boy up, trying to comfort him. "You'll come up to the country with us—" he was saying when the line went dead.

Of course: There would be no way to get back into the city. Michael would have to take Nick to our little cottage in upstate New York.

In the conference room, the television was still on and I watched, horrified, as the first tower crumbled. We'd had regular fire drills but were unprepared for a catastrophe of this magnitude, and Human Resources, usually so capable, could not be reached.

"You okay?" Gina came by to say that she was leaving. Downtown was being evacuated. We hugged each other, unsure when—if—we'd see each other again.

Phone lines were down, communication impossible, and people were desperate to find their families. As they wandered the halls in shock and I made sure everyone had a plan and a place, time slowed to a crawl. It seemed as if hours passed before I picked up my purse and made one last circuit through the now-empty office. Then, at last, I headed home.

Outside, frightened people stumbled through Times Square. Above us the neon lights blinked, eerily incongruous. The air had turned a vicious yellow and was filled with an acrid, unfamiliar stench. Subways weren't running, bank machines were empty, and as I raced uptown, moving as fast as I could, I found streets blocked by abandoned cars that seemed to have simply run out of gas. I remembered, gratefully, that my own tank was full.

"They say they've closed the bridges." The super, who was running the elevator, was always a source of grim news.

"Something must be open," I said. "There must be some way to get out." I ran into the apartment and scooped up two terrified cats. The dirty dishes were still sitting in the sink and I inhaled the familiar scent—bacon and orange juice—wondering if we'd ever be back. At the last minute, I snatched up our passports. You never knew.

By now every vehicle in Manhattan was on the road, desperate to escape. Fighter jets screeched overhead. Sirens blared. Blinding sun glared off the roofs of the unmoving river of cars. The cats yowled. On an ordinary day, the trip to the Henry Hudson Bridge at Manhattan's northern tip takes ten minutes; today it took four agonizing hours. But the bridge, when I reached it, was open.

On the other side the air grew clearer, the day stranger. The weather was radiant, and as I drove farther north through green countryside, watching cows placidly munch grass beneath a clear blue sky, it was hard to believe what lay behind me. An hour later, as I pulled into our driveway, I found Michael tossing a ball with a group of children.

"The school just let you take them?"

"They were happy for any option, glad to be able to tell parents their kids were safely out of the city. Nobody knows what's coming next. We watched TV for a while when we got here, but the news was making the kids so nervous that I brought them all outside."

For the rest of their lives, I thought, these kids will remember exactly where they were when the towers came down.

I made spaghetti, and we all listened for the ring of the phone as we ate. One by one the parents checked in, and by bedtime we knew that we were among the lucky ones: Nobody here had lost a relative.

We woke to another eerily radiant day. Parents arrived to claim their kids; our friend John, Julia's dad, had rented a car in Chicago and driven through the night. He hugged his daughter to him and then tumbled gratefully into bed.

The news was terrible; we all knew people who had been in the Twin Towers, and we sat glued to the television, desperately hoping they had survived. But the immediate danger seemed to have passed; firefighters were pouring into the city, the bridges slowly being reopened. I wandered disconsolately around the house, spooked by this freakishly ordinary country day. Impulsively, I grabbed my car keys.

"I can't stay here," I said. "I'm going back."

Nobody seemed to hear me.

"Back to the city." I spoke louder. "They're letting people in again. We've got eight kitchens at *Gourmet*. And somebody's got to feed the firefighters."

Michael didn't miss a beat. "We'll come too," he said.

Memo to All *Gourmet* Staff

The magazine is closed until further notice. But our kitchens are standing idle. . . . This is not a command performance, but I'm going to 4 Times Square to cook for the workers at Ground Zero, and you're welcome to join me. Buy some groceries and meet me in the morning. It may not be much, but it's what we can do.

Then I put in a call to Drew Nieporent, the largest personality in the restaurant world, figuring he'd have a plan. When Drew opened Montrachet in 1985, it was the first high-end restaurant in the area that would soon become Tribeca, and he now owned a handful of iconic restaurants that had once stood in the shadow of the Twin Towers: Nobu, Tribeca Grill, Zeppole. Yes, he said, of course he was planning on feeding the rescue workers. We agreed that my crew—whoever they turned out to be—would cook all day and then meet him downtown so we could distribute our food together.

My expectations were low; people were busy comforting their families, and I thought a mere handful of the staff would show up. But when I walked into the kitchens at 9:00 A.M., the place was packed. Word had gone out—Drew, of course—and people were desperate to help. A restaurant PR person showed up with her parents, an ad salesman from *GQ* came with his kids, and one of the sales reps brought his entire family. In this mad mix of food lovers, half were strangers.

I channeled my inner Larry: You should send everyone who's not staff away. There are insurance issues. What if someone cuts off his finger? What if someone sues?

Then I silenced the voice: The regular rules did not apply. I cranked up the music, and as the kitchens filled with the scent of chili and chocolate, we began to dance, defiant in the face of disaster.

We all knew why we were there, knew it was as much for ourselves as for the firefighters, knew we were attempting to snatch hope from the rubble of our broken city. And food was the perfect way to do it.

Around five we packed great trays of chili, cornbread, lasagna, and brownies into coolers, loaded them into my van, and headed downtown. We passed a checkpoint at 23rd Street and another at 14th. Down here it was all dust and rubble, growing thicker with each passing block. By the time we reached Canal Street, the streets were no longer passable, and we abandoned the van, shouldered the chests of food, and headed to meet Drew at Montrachet.

We weren't the only ones feeding the rescue workers; chefs from all over the city set up makeshift kitchens around the disaster. But we were the only ones who took our food right into the heart of Ground Zero, and although we'd seen it on television, nothing had prepared us for this horror. It was a bombed-out war zone, a zombie space that no longer resembled any New York I'd ever known.

Near what had once been Reade Street, a fireman handed out face masks, and we tied them on and marched in, tripping over hoses with our cases of food. Above us the surviving skyscrapers tilted at uncomfortable angles, staring vacantly down through blackened holes that had once been windows.

Lured by the scent of chili and cornbread, exhausted firefighters came stumbling out of the dust. Covered in white powder, they were like ghosts staggering through the smoke.

"Is that chili?" A man collapsed onto a broken beam and pulled off his respirator; his mouth gleamed beneath the ashen grime of his face as he fell upon the food.

It wasn't much; it was a bowl of chili. But when the man looked up and said, "Thank you for this taste of home," I looked around at the dust and smoke and chaos and began to cry.

I remembered that moment a week later, when I sat down to write the monthly Letter from the Editor.

"We were almost finished with this Thanksgiving issue," I began, "when the world fell apart." Then I stopped; it had been only seven days since the Twin Towers came down, and none of us knew what lay ahead. I was writing into a vacuum. "Because monthly magazines are written long before they actually appear on your doorstep, I have no idea what life will be like when you read these words." It was the first time that I understood, really understood, that the world would never be the same.

I thought about my own Thanksgiving, wondering what it would be like this year. I heard the firefighter's voice once again and realized that in the rubble of the World Trade Center I'd suddenly understood the true meaning of food. I knew, without any doubt, that as long as I lived, chili would be one of the ways in which I offer thanks.

Thanksgiving, of course, isn't Thanksgiving without turkey. So my Thanksgiving chili is a turkey version based on a beloved Gourmet *recipe. I made it in 2001, and since then our Thanksgiving table has never been without it. It reminds us, sadly, of the friends we lost on 9/11—and of the many reasons we have to be thankful.*

THANKSGIVING TURKEY CHILI

• • •

1 tablespoon cumin seeds

3 canned whole chipotle chilies
   in adobo

1 bottle dark beer

2 pounds tomatillos (husked,
   rinsed, and quartered)

3 tablespoons vegetable oil

3 large onions (chopped)

½ cup fresh cilantro (chopped)

2 teaspoons fresh oregano
   (finely minced)

2 jalapeños (diced; if you don't
   like heat, remove the seeds)

3½ pounds ground turkey

1½ cups chicken broth

8 large cloves of garlic (peeled
   but left whole)

Salt

1 bay leaf

2 cups cooked white beans

1 4-ounce can diced green
   chile peppers

Cream sherry

Balsamic vinegar

Sour cream

Toast the cumin seeds in a dry skillet until they're fragrant. Allow to cool, then grind to powder.

Puree the chipotle chilies with the adobo.

Put the beer into a medium-sized pot, add the tomatillos, bring to a boil, and turn the heat down to a simmer. Cook for about five minutes, until the tomatillos are soft. Strain the tomatillos (reserving liquid), and puree in a blender or food processor. Pour back into the pot with the beer.

Slick the bottom of a large casserole with a couple of tablespoons of oil, and sauté the onions until they're translucent. Add the cilantro, oregano, jalapeños, and cumin and stir for a couple of minutes. Break the turkey into the mixture and stir until it just starts to lose its raw color. Add the pureed tomatillos and beer, the chipotle puree, the chicken broth, and the garlic, along with a couple of teaspoons of salt and the bay leaf, and simmer the mixture for about an hour and a half.

With a large spoon, smash the now-soft cloves of garlic and stir them into the chili. Add the white beans and diced chile peppers and taste for salt. At this point I like to start playing with the flavors, adding a few splashes of cream sherry, a bit of balsamic vinegar, or perhaps some soy or fish sauce. Heat for another 10 minutes.

Serve with sour cream.

Serves 8

17

FOOD PEOPLE

ON THE MORNING OF SEPTEMBER 11, MICHAEL LOMONACO, THE CHEF of Windows on the World, broke his glasses during breakfast service. He took the long ride down from the 107th floor to have them repaired, stepping out of the elevator just as the first plane hit. He stood on the ground as the building crumbled and the seventy-nine cooks, waiters, and dishwashers he had just left vanished. As he painfully made his way uptown, he couldn't stop thinking about the families his colleagues had left behind, and he determined to do something to help them. The whole food world pitched in, and within a month they'd raised twenty-three million dollars.

After the World Trade Center attacks, New Yorkers who survived asked a single question: How can we help? Everyone went into action, parties were canceled, and food people mobilized to feed the rescue workers who poured in from across the country.

We were proud of ourselves, but as the weather grew colder

this constant mourning began to feel like defeat. We had to get back to normal life, if only to prove that the enemy had not won. At *Gourmet* we'd canceled our September gala celebrating the magazine's sixtieth anniversary, but by December a party seemed not only welcome but necessary, a display of defiance.

The whole city was ready to dance, and people showed up at the Whitney Museum dressed to the nines in an almost desperate party mood. I stood in the middle of the swirling crowd, watching the guests eat and drink with the abandon of survivors. Maurie's people had cajoled celebrities into coming, and they made sure I was photographed with each famous face; as the hours wore on, my own grew tight from smiling.

Around midnight, when the party ended, I stood outside, saying wistfully to Laurie, "I wish we didn't have to go home. That was all business and now I'm ready for some fun." Chef Daniel Boulud was standing nearby, and he whipped out his phone. Punching in numbers, he began pacing up and down on the sidewalk in front of the museum, issuing orders in rapid French. He stopped and put his hand over the receiver to ask, *"Vous êtes combien de personnes?"*

I looked around, embarrassed; the staff numbered sixty-five. And there were spouses. Friends. Chefs.

"Uh . . ." I hesitated. It was such a huge number.

Daniel looked impatient. *"Je vous invite,"* he said.

"A hundred people?" I whispered it reluctantly.

"Disons cent cinquante," he said into the phone. I imagined what they must be thinking over at Restaurant Daniel. A party for one hundred fifty? At the end of service? On the spur of the moment? A party that would include every major chef and food writer in the city? This could not be welcome news.

But Daniel continued issuing orders into the phone. I heard, *"Pâté. Saumon. Fromage. Patisserie."*

The Whitney Museum was less than a mile from Restaurant Daniel, but by the time we arrived, the tables in the private salon sported crisp white tablecloths and a vast buffet stretched across the back of the room. Waiters circulated with champagne.

The word had gone out, and with each hour more chefs showed up. Sometime in the early morning—was it three or four?—I looked around at all those people who'd pitched in when the city was in trouble. As a fledgling food writer for a small San Francisco magazine, I'd spent a lot of time with the young chefs who were creating an entirely new American profession, and now I realized how much I'd missed their company. Educated, articulate, and passionate about their craft, they were unlike the generation that had come before them, and during my tenure as a critic I'd missed their lively minds, their creativity, and their enormous generosity.

"This has given me an idea!" Karen Danick, *Gourmet*'s director of media relations, stood before me, flute of champagne in her hand. Karen could not have been more than thirty-five, but she was old-school, a traditional PR person out of central casting. A large woman, she arrived each morning in a dense cloud of perfume, sporting a perennial tan, very high heels, tight black Lycra dresses, and copious amounts of makeup. Her voice was never pitched at less than maximum volume, and she ended every sentence with an exclamation point.

"What if we threw a party like this every few months? After hours! Just for chefs! It would be a way of giving back to them!"

Karen's chef parties became a *Gourmet* hallmark. They didn't start till midnight and they went on until the last reveler—usually the sweet, younger, not-yet-famous Tony Bourdain—staggered into the dawn. Everyone came. People sang and talked and ate. People danced on the tables. People drank.

I loved every one of those parties, but the one I remember best is the one we threw just after Si made one of his rare visits to my office.

He'd sidled in the door, face slightly flushed with what I later understood was embarrassment, and lowered himself into the seat on the far side of my desk. Leaning over, he whispered, "You're going to have a new publisher."

I was too stunned to say anything—I'd had no warning—and Si shifted uncomfortably in his chair. "We're giving Gina a start-up." He looked out the window, down at the desk, anywhere but in my direction. "*Teen Vogue*. She wants to build something from the ground up, something of her own. She's earned that right."

"Who's coming to *Gourmet*?"

Again, he did not meet my eyes. "We're bringing in Giulio Capua. He's been the associate publisher of *GQ* for a long time, and he's due for a promotion. But we had to give *GQ* to Ron Galotti, so we looked around for something else for Giulio."

It was hardly an enthusiastic endorsement, but Florio, ever the consummate pitchman, followed up. Minutes after Si left my office, Steve was on the phone, selling me on my new publisher. "You'll love Giulio!" he gushed. "He's a real talent, and I know you two are going to do fantastic things together!

"Art Cooper," he confided sotto voce, a secret for my ears alone, "is devastated to be losing Giulio." He painted a picture of the legendary *GQ* editor in chief, begging not to be deprived of his beloved AP. "But this," Florio finished triumphantly, "is Giulio's chance, his shot at the big time, and he's going to knock himself out to show us what he can do. And *you're* going to get the benefit of all that energy!" He'd saved a final parting shot. "You're a seasoned editor now, so you can mold him in whatever way you want. Wait and see; you're going to be *thrilled* by this change."

I had no idea what to expect; none of the Condé Nast publishers I'd met were cut from the same cloth. Some, like the legendary

Ron Galotti (widely believed to be the model for *Sex and the City*'s Mr. Big), were as brash and flashy as Florio himself. *The New Yorker*'s David Carey was quietly brilliant, *Vanity Fair*'s Pete Hunsinger the epitome of a gentleman, and *Men's Vogue*'s William Li the personification of hip elegance. When I met Giulio later that morning, he turned out to be different from all of them. Lithe and athletic, with strongly defined features and deep-black eyes, he was as striking as a figure on an ancient Roman coin. He introduced himself and immediately started talking about food.

"You cook?" I was incredulous. Gina was so uncomfortable in the kitchen that the one time she'd attempted to make dinner, she set the oven on fire. "I'd never used it before," she said indignantly. "How was I supposed to know they'd leave the instruction book inside?"

"I'm Italian." Giulio shrugged, as if that said it all, and continued discussing recipes. It was a savvy charm offensive, but it worked; delighted by the notion of a publisher who cooked, I said impulsively, "We're having a party tonight. Why don't you come to Chef's Night Out?"

"I'd like that," he said. "I've spent my business life among fashion people, and I'm curious about this new world I'm about to step into."

This party was at Eleven Madison Park, and chef Kerry Heffernan had outdone himself. The food was interesting and inventive and the liquor flowed. Around three in the morning, Giulio came looking for me. By then we were all disheveled, but his suit was as neat as if he'd just removed it from the closet, and if he'd been drinking he could certainly hold his liquor.

His face, however, glowed. "My mind is blown!" He pointed across the room, where Mario Batali was standing with Daniel Boulud and Eric Ripert.

I didn't understand.

"They're together," he said. "Talking."

"So?"

"Mario just told Eric he has a kid in the kitchen at Babbo who should be working at Le Bernardin. He said he was going to send him over tomorrow."

"Chefs do that all the time. They send their most talented kids to *stage* with other chefs so they can gain experience."

Giulio shook his head. "You don't get it, do you?"

"Get what?"

"What an amazing world you live in. I'm used to fashion people. Do you think Ralph Lauren and Donna Karan would even be in the same room together? Food people are a different species."

This was, of course, before the #MeToo moment tore down the curtain and exposed the ugliness behind the kitchen door. How much did we know? I'd been writing articles since the seventies about the rise of the woman chef, and I'd heard the stories about the old days. But I'd thought that was behind us.

Still, if I'm being honest, I have to admit that working women everywhere accepted casual misogyny. We were so accustomed to taking what men dished out that we thought it was up to us to find ways to deflect the advances of bosses and co-workers without hurting their feelings. As someone who spent many years in restaurants as a waitress, cook, and writer, I can't say that the chefs I met were any worse than the men I encountered in publishing or the art world. In retrospect I feel like a coward for having put up with any of that, but it was what we all considered the way of the world. I hope my granddaughters will live in a better one.

At the time, my only thought was that Giulio was a quick study; in one night he'd intuited everything that enchanted me about the restaurant world. When I first started writing, there were only a handful of us—men and women—who were interested in food and wine, but we felt we were in it together. There had been no boundaries, no distinction between writers and chefs, and I'd felt part of a close community intent on improving the way America eats. Back in the seventies the food world was so amorphous that, when I was reporting a long piece about the opening of Michael's Restaurant in Santa Monica, Michael McCarty had asked, seriously, if I had any money to invest in his restaurant. I didn't, of course, but it was a sign of how loosely the lines were drawn.

All that changed when I became the restaurant critic of *The New York Times*. I didn't know any New York chefs and I couldn't get to know them. I was the enemy, the person whose picture hung behind the swinging kitchen doors with WANTED written across the bottom in giant letters.

I hadn't realized how much I'd missed them. But I was very happy to be home.

18

ENORMOUS CHANGES

WHEN LAURIE MENTIONED, WITH STUDIED CASUALNESS, THAT SHE had thought of the perfect person to replace her if the time should ever come, I was completely unsuspecting.

"Who?" A good manager, after all, needs a contingency plan.

"John Willoughby. Do you know him?"

I'd met the editor of *Cook's Illustrated* at least a dozen times, but I could hardly say I knew him. "You sure?" I said. Tall and striking, Willoughby had bright-silver hair, startlingly blue eyes, and the cool elegance of a New England Brahmin. "He always kind of frightens me."

"I can see why." Laurie, aware of my deep aversion to change, did not mention why she had brought this up. "But I taught a food-writing class with him, and beneath that aristocratic manner is a smart man with a generous soul. The students were all in love with him. You should invite him to New York and spend some time with him."

Why not? I thought, putting in the call. It would be good to be prepared, should we ever have an opening. Willoughby, however, did not seem thrilled when I asked him to come for an interview. He agreed to make the trip from Boston, but I had the distinct impression that he had little interest in a new job. "I've been longing to visit the Condé Nast cafeteria," he admitted.

Si would have been pleased; this was exactly why he'd lured Frank Gehry to 4 Times Square. The cafeteria might masquerade as the company canteen, but Si had wanted to create New York's most exclusive club.

It was a singularly brilliant move, and it worked exactly as planned. The cafeteria got so much press that the whole world yearned to visit Gehry's soaring space with its sinuous glass panels and curving titanium walls. The fact that an invitation was required made it that much more enticing.

For prospective employees, the cafeteria was always an attraction. This was fine with me; I like interviewing people over lunch. You can learn a lot about people by watching them eat, and I wondered what I'd glean from my meal with John.

He walked in and looked around, seeming suitably impressed. He pointed to the Chinese-food line, where a famous actor was waiting. "Is that . . . ?"

On any given day, the Condé Nast cafeteria was packed with celebrities whose agents had wrangled invitations. John slipped in behind the star and watched a cook toss tough nuggets of precooked chicken into a wok, add some limp, overcooked vegetables, and smother it all with garlic-free kung pao sauce. Tugging on his apron, the cook gave the mess a listless stir. "That looks dreadful," said John, easing out of the line.

I herded him toward the sushi station, where "sushi chefs" were arranging presliced fish onto soggy seaweed. The skinny *Vogue* assistant in front of us leaned in to negotiate.

"Will you please cut my tuna roll in twelve?" she asked the chef.

"Eight!" he said curtly.

"Please." She actually batted her eyelashes. "Please cut it into twelve. For me. I'm on a diet and it makes it seem like more."

John gave a shout of laughter and edged out of the line to move on to the steam table, where a pair of *GQ* editors were earnestly discussing the merits of lukewarm fried chicken. He shadowed them as they surveyed a vast tray of macaroni paved in a thick orange crust. "I'd bet my life that's not Velveeta!" said one.

John looked at the oozing tray and shuddered slightly. "But everyone says the food here is good!" His disappointment was palpable.

Only those who haven't eaten here, I started to say, but prudently kept my mouth shut. You never knew who might be listening. "They make pretty good sandwiches," I ventured, pointing to the interns jockeying for position in front of two white-coated workers. The men were conducting a frantic competition to see who could cram the most protein between two slices of bread, and John watched, mesmerized, as one stuffed a pound of bacon onto a single sandwich, then added a heap of tomatoes, a mountain of lettuce, and an entire avocado. Wrapping the towering concoction into white paper, he penciled "BLT" across the front and with a wink handed it across the counter.

"They know the interns aren't paid," I whispered, "but watch this." The next customer, an older executive, ordered a Brie-and-prosciutto sandwich. The cook nodded briefly, picked up a dainty croissant, sliced it in two, inserted a sliver of cheese and a single slice of ham, and passed it across the counter. No wink.

"That," said John, "is democracy in action."

"Yeah," I said. "I guess the counter guys figure anyone who spends twelve bucks on a sandwich doesn't need their help."

As I spoke, Si began to wriggle out of his booth on the far side of the room. I tugged on John's sleeve. "C'mon. Hurry!"

Our timing was perfect.

We followed at a discreet distance as Si trotted through the cafeteria with his tray. John stared, rapt, as Si carefully separated the dirty plates and glasses. "I never knew," he said, "how satisfying it could be to watch a billionaire bus his own dishes." He gave me a sidelong glance. "But would you mind very much if we ate somewhere else?"

He'd aced the first part of the interview.

We rode the subway downtown and John stretched his long legs into the aisle, seeming comfortable. He did not ask why we weren't in a limo, but he looked at me with those startling eyes and said, "My friends all call me Doc. I wish you would too."

"Have you always been called that?"

"Just since college. I grew up in Iowa, and I was such a bumpkin my roommate said I reminded him of a country doctor. The name kind of stuck."

"What college?"

He hesitated, looking so abashed that I was completely unprepared for the answer.

"Harvard." He sounded embarrassed. I glanced at him with some surprise; every other Harvard person I've ever met has managed to drop the name in the first five minutes.

How could I not like him?

When we walked into Pearl Oyster Bar, Doc studied the small, modest restaurant with its long marble counter and took a deep breath. It smelled like clams, like lemons, like lobsters. "I was afraid"—he sank happily onto a stool—"you were going to take me to some stuffy uptown restaurant. This is perfect."

We started with fried oysters, and I plucked one from my plate, showered it with fresh lemon juice, took a bite. The outside crackled gently before yielding to the small, savory custard inside. It was like eating sea foam, and I closed my eyes to better experience the pleasure. When I opened them, Doc was watching me. I silently handed him an oyster.

"Wine?" I asked. He nodded, and we listened to the clear pale liquid rush into our glasses. We clinked, the merry sound a nod to the simple goodness of the food.

Lobsters arrived and we tore into them with our fingers, teasing out the rich meat of the tail, the subtle smoothness of the claws. We were eating silently, sucking on the little swimmerets to extract every bit of meat. He seemed to feel no need to talk, no need to sell himself. An odd interview, perhaps, but it had told me everything I needed to know. He wasn't Laurie, but if the time ever came, we'd work well together.

Salad then, a perfect Caesar, each crisp leaf of romaine reveling in its anchovy-laced dressing. Doc matched me bite for bite, and we did not leave a single crouton.

"Dessert?" I asked.

We shared a butterscotch praline sundae; he ate most of it. He was, I thought, a modest man with an appreciation for pleasure.

"I don't have an opening now," I said when he put his spoon down. I was still clueless. "But I'd love to work with you someday."

"It would be tempting," he conceded. "But . . ." He gestured toward the window. Outside, people were hurrying past, heads bent into the wind on the gritty Village street. "This would be a huge change, and I like my life now. Do I really want to give up everything I know to move to New York?"

I understood exactly how he felt.

"SO YOU LIKED HIM?" LOOKING relieved, Laurie finally revealed that she'd been asked to run the *LA Weekly*. "Editor in chief!" She looked apologetic. "I started my career there and I just can't turn it down." She reached out a hand, touched my arm. "It won't be such a big change," she promised. "We'll still see lots of each other. Jonathan's going to stay on as *Gourmet*'s restaurant critic, so we'll be bicoastal."

"But it won't be the same!" Laurie was leaving and the change loomed, leaving me feeling frightened and betrayed. I'd liked Doc Willoughby, but who was he really? A silver-haired stranger who might turn out to be anyone at all.

19

JUST SAY IT

I GAVE DOC A COPY OF E. B. WHITE'S *HERE IS NEW YORK* AS A WEL-
come gift, but he didn't need it; he fell in love with the city—and
with *Gourmet*—on day one. He slid so seamlessly into our lives that
it hardly felt like change. After the first few weeks, none of us
could remember a time he hadn't been there. Smart, forthright,
and kind, he had the remarkable ability to say exactly what he
thought, no matter how negative, without ever seeming hostile.
He was always firm, but in seven years I never saw him lose his
temper. Larry liked him immediately, and although he never said
so, I thought he was relieved I'd chosen someone more conventional than Laurie. As for the staff, they adored him.

I missed Laurie, missed her calm presence and her brilliant
editing instincts. I missed our forays to the far corners of the city
to eat strange dishes none of our friends would touch. But the
hard part was behind us; *Gourmet* was thriving, and our readers
now seemed eager for increasingly challenging content. It was

thrilling. And in an odd way, her leaving liberated me: I had weathered an enormous change, and it had proved painless.

But it was more than that. The *Gourmet* staff was now a solid team working seamlessly together, and Laurie's leaving hadn't changed that. I admired every one of the people I worked with, and I was proud of the magazine we were making. Now, for the first time, I acknowledged that it wasn't just luck and it wasn't an accident; I had actually spearheaded this. It made me very proud.

My new publisher was also promising, although I did have early doubts about Giulio's competence. The first time he took me on an ad call, he looked askance when I asked who we were supposed to be.

I reminded myself that he was new at this game. "I'm asking what you want me to tell these ad reps about *Gourmet*," I said patiently. "Are we a lifestyle book or a travel book? Upscale or down-to-earth? Should I talk about the recipes? You need to give me marching orders."

"Why go through all that?" He sounded genuinely perplexed. "Just explain your vision. We're *Gourmet,* and that speaks for itself."

I studied him warily. In Gina's world we had tried to figure out what the clients wanted to hear—and then made sure that they did. "I don't know," I began. "It seems kind of risky. Especially since you're new and ad sales are bound to slump for a few months."

"They'll come back," he said, with what I considered unearned assurance. I'd learned by then how personal ad sales are, and I knew that many of Gina's accounts would follow her out the door. As a first-time publisher, Giulio would not be bringing old accounts along, and we were certain to suffer.

But he appeared to be unconcerned. "All you need to do is tell them your vision for the magazine."

"That's all?"

"Preview some upcoming articles, talk about why you're publishing them. That's all I ask; the rest is my job."

I was uneasy and he sensed my discomfort. "This is how I see it." He was so earnest. "On paper we look exactly like the competition. I can massage the figures a bit, but people aren't fooled—we have the same demographics as all the other food and travel books. What's different about us is our content. Nobody's ever produced an epicurean magazine like this before; that's what we have to get across."

But getting anything across to ad reps is extremely difficult. They're trained to have no affect, and no matter how fast you talk or how many jokes you tell, they sit like stones, giving nothing back.

This group was no different. "I tried everything," I told Nick and Michael later. "When I told about sending Bruce Feiler off with a pocketful of cash to buy his way into hot restaurants, it almost worked. One of the reps actually asked a question."

"What?" Nick wanted to know.

"He asked if Bruce had tried it at a Danny Meyer restaurant. When I said a twenty-dollar bill slipped to the maître d' snagged an instant table at Union Square on a busy Saturday night, there was an actual gasp. Then the room went quiet; they were embarrassed that I'd tricked them into reacting."

"But will they buy an ad?" Michael wanted to know.

"We'll have to wait and see. But I worry that Giulio likes the magazine too much to be an effective salesman. The other day he brought his mother in. Can you imagine? She's this lovely, very shy old lady, and she's saved all her *Gourmets* going back to the fifties. When I took her down to the test kitchen, I thought she would faint from happiness. It was very sweet."

"Don't underestimate that man," said Michael. "He knows

exactly how to charm you. He just has a different set of tools than Gina. But I bet when you want to publish a serious investigative report he's going to give you that same old line about not offending the readers."

Edgy articles had always made Gina nervous, but Giulio was different. When I showed him Barry Estabrook's article on the horrors of salmon farms, he was positively enthusiastic. The accepted wisdom was that fish farms were going to save the world, but Barry reported that they were just another form of animal factory, polluting the water, creating dead zones on the ocean floor, and filling the fish with antibiotics.

"Farmed salmon don't even have orange flesh," I said, showing Giulio the color wheel Barry had sent with the article. "But nobody wants to eat an ugly gray salmon, so the farmers feed them color pellets. These are the various shades of orange they can choose from."

Giulio gave the wheel a spin. "Our advertising partners eat salmon too," he said. "They'll want to know this." Later he sent me a note laying out his thinking. "As I see it, this is a win-win. The affluent epicures who already subscribe will be grateful; they want to know what's in the salmon they're buying. But younger readers are going to be especially interested; this is the kind of story that will make them realize this isn't their grandmother's *Gourmet* anymore. Stories like this set us apart."

I hoped he was right, but I was not convinced. As Christmas approached I noted, with growing trepidation, that ad sales were not improving. I dreaded yet another new publisher; who knew who they'd send next?

Christmas at Condé Nast meant the annual Four Seasons lunch—and the annual speculation about who would be seated where. The press parsed the iconography as if it were the Last Supper. According to the accepted wisdom, sitting with Si was an excellent omen, and a seat near Truman or Florio was a sure sign of favor. Maurie's table, on the other hand, was considered bad luck; it was widely believed to mean that this was your last lunch.

I was relieved to be seated next to Si. But as soon as I sat down, I began to fret: What on earth was I going to say once he'd finished his holiday remarks?

He stood and stammered to a start, launching into a speech so disjointed I began to fear he'd drift off in the middle and simply stare into space. Then, amazingly, his cadence changed, picking up speed as he proudly enumerated the year's achievements. Circulation was soaring, ad revenues rocketing, and his pride was so palpable that as he rambled to a close someone at the next table murmured, "Si certainly seems pleased with himself."

"Why not?" It was a publisher I didn't recognize, making no attempt to keep her voice down. "We blew past Hachette, we blew past Hearst, and now we're right on the heels of Time Inc. *The New Yorker*'s stopped hemorrhaging money, and all the people who laughed at Si are being forced to eat their words."

I was grateful to the anonymous publisher; I now knew exactly what to say. "It's really a pleasure," I began as Si sat down, "to be working for a company that trusts the intelligence of its readers. I think you're the only American publisher who does. You must be proud it's finally paying off."

He looked at me for such a long time that I wondered if I'd overstepped. At last he nodded. "Yes," he said, stabbing a fork through the crust of his chicken potpie; it shattered with a satisfying crack.

I looked around, searching out Giulio, hoping he'd noticed where I was seated. When I finally found him—at Maurie's table—all the pleasure drained out of me. He was apparently among the doomed.

Christmas presents were always delivered while we were at

lunch, and Robin was waiting with undisguised impatience to see what Si's card said. Extracting it from the envelope, she read Si's large, spiky script: "'I have the greatest regard for the fine magazine you're making.'"

"Is that good or bad?" I was still clueless when it came to deciphering the inscrutable Condé Nast code.

"Very good."

She handed me a small turquoise box tied with a big white bow. "This one's from Florio."

"Do you know what it is?"

She smiled. "Take it home and let Nick open it; I think he'll like it."

What, I wondered, could Tiffany possibly produce to thrill a thirteen-year-old boy?

"COOL!" SAID NICK WHEN I handed him the box at dinner. Untying the ribbon, he extracted a soft felt bag with TIFFANY & CO. printed on the flap. When he gave it a shake, a shiny silver object came tumbling out. Nick held it in the palm of his hand, staring down at his reflection.

"A yo-yo?" Michael was incredulous. "Steve Florio sent you a sterling silver yo-yo?"

"Cool!" Nick said again.

Michael made a strangled sound. Nick and I both turned to look at him.

"What's wrong?" I asked as Nick stared down at the gleaming yo-yo as if it held a secret he was trying to decode.

Michael looked at me. "Do I really have to spell it out?"

I regarded the lustrous toy, and then I reached over, took the thing out of Nick's hand, slid it back into the fuzzy blue bag, and set it in its box. The turquoise cube sat on the table, throbbing color as we all stared at it. For a moment no one spoke. Then the phone began to ring, and with a look of enormous relief Nick ran to get it.

"It's for you, Mom." He handed me the receiver, mouthing, "Florio."

There was no preamble, and Florio didn't beat around the bush. "It's Giulio." His voice was crisp, carrying none of its usual ingratiating charm. "His numbers aren't good, and we think we made a mistake. We brought him along too fast."

"What are you saying?"

"He's not ready. We thought he could be a publisher, but we were wrong. We want to get you someone more seasoned, but before I make the change, I wanted to check with you."

"It's only been a few months. . . ." I began. "Don't you think you should give him a chance?"

"If that's what you want." Florio was all business. "Merry Christmas."

Michael said nothing. Nick was quiet. The silence grew as they stared resolutely at their plates. "Say it," I said. "Whatever it is. Just say it."

They looked at each other. Michael cleared his throat. "Are you sure you should have done that?"

"Why not?"

"Now it's on your shoulders." He pointed at the turquoise box as if it contained all of Condé Nast. "If the numbers keep going down, Giulio's not going to be the only one who fails. It's going to be your fault too."

20

HELLO, CUPCAKE

WHEN DIANA STRODE INTO MY OFFICE TO ANNOUNCE THAT SHE TOO was leaving, all my fears came roaring back. Laurie had gone. Gina had gone. Giulio was in trouble. And now Diana was walking out the door.

"Why?" I moaned. Even to my own ears I sounded like a child.

"I've decided to retire. I've got enough money saved, the book's running smoothly, and it's time for me to go."

"I warned you," said Truman. "Diana gets restless. She enjoys creating new things and fixing broken ones. *Gourmet*'s not new, it's no longer broken, and the day-to-day operations pose no challenges to her." He gave me a searching look, saw my fear, and misunderstood. "You can't take it personally," he said.

There was no point in trying to explain. But as a parade of art directors trooped through my office, I grew increasingly uneasy. I met talented art directors, pleasant art directors, creative art directors—but none of them inspired me as Diana had done. She had given *Gourmet* a signature look, and none of them struck me as capable of building on it. On the dreary, rainy afternoon when Robin ushered the latest candidate in, I was in despair.

The man was slight, so thin that the large black umbrella he clutched looked like it weighed more than he did. In the other hand he carried an enormous portfolio, which seemed to be tugging him forward like an impatient dog. Richard Ferretti dripped across the office, brushed back his long black hair, and joined me at the table.

He slid his résumé in front of me, and I sighed as I examined a long list of clients from Coach to Revlon. Although it included many magazines, they were all in the past, so I began with the obvious question: "Why would you want to go back to working at a magazine?"

"I don't want to work at a magazine." As he smoothed back the strands of shiny blue-black hair, I wondered how old he was. His lean, intelligent face seemed much younger than his résumé indicated. "I want to work at *Gourmet.*"

"Why?"

He looked directly at me, startling me with the intensity of his gaze. "Because I love to cook and I like what you're doing here. But the visuals could be so much stronger. You need to take more chances."

When I just stared at him, he rose, went over to the rack of back issues, and extracted a few. Opening the first to the big "*Gourmet* Entertains" centerfold, he threw it down before me. Then he did the same with the others. "The food's beautiful." He gestured at an elegantly set table. "Often the setting is too. But that's it. These are random pictures of pretty food. And it would be so much more powerful if you were telling stories."

Pulling out a notebook, he began to sketch. "We could create a script for every menu and shoot it like a movie. Nobody's ever done that, but think about how much more exciting it would be. You'd be able to imagine yourself sitting at the table with these people, know what their relationships were and what they were talking about. We could invite the readers to join us at a party every month."

This is what went through my mind: Why didn't I think of that? What else did this extraordinary person have to teach me?

"There's so much you could be doing!" He got up, so animated now that a force field seemed to surround him. "All the food magazines use the same photographers. Why limit yourself when there are so many other talented people? What if we used photographers who have never shot food before? Think how different they'd make everything look; it would give us a whole new perspective."

"And what else?"

"I'd like to shoot a real party, in real time."

This was ridiculous. Our photo shoots required weeks of preparation; we arrived at each location with at least two versions of every dish, along with extra plates and props. We chose the models, coordinated their clothes, spent hours setting up lights and considering angles. "You'd never have enough time to shoot a real party in natural light. It would get dark; the food would get cold; people would look wrong. You'd miss most of it."

"We might." He was matter-of-fact. "On the other hand, we might get something extraordinary. We could hire news photographers; they're used to shooting fast, no second chances. If it worked, we'd end up with a kind of immediacy that would set it apart from every other food shoot you've ever seen. Why not try? It could be amazing!"

Richard was just getting started; he overflowed with ideas. "I'd like to work with the cooks, think about the visuals as they're developing the recipes. Afterward is too late. And I've always wanted to shoot a meal that looks like one of those Dutch master paintings."

The light outside faded. When Doc poked his head in to say good night, Richard and I were sitting in the dark, still talking, the words spilling from our mouths. "You've been taking risks, and there's nothing more difficult. But I think you need to push the envelope even more."

I glanced at my watch; we'd been talking for hours, and there was still so much to say. Reluctantly, I stood. "My family will be starving; I need to go home and cook dinner."

"I need to go too," he said, but we stood for a moment, wistfully regarding each other. Working with him, I thought, would be an adventure.

"You can't afford Richard Ferretti." Truman said it flatly. "He's got his own business and he makes a lot of money."

"I think he might come anyway." I was absurdly optimistic. Truman shook his head, loath to disappoint me. He was visibly surprised when Richard said yes, and I was so excited that I began taking risks even before he came on board.

Whose idea was it to hire Matthew Rolston, famous for his *Rolling Stone* covers, to shoot our restaurant issue? Who thought of gathering a group of chefs and posing them like rock stars? I don't remember. What I do remember is the excitement at the magazine as we began planning the cover.

The band we ultimately assembled featured the country's hottest chefs playing "instruments" constructed out of kitchen utensils. Dallas chef Dean Fearing, who was then at the Mansion on Turtle Creek, strutted with a "guitar" made out of spatulas, pot lids, cooling racks, and pastry tips, as did Laurent Gras (he'd left Alain Ducasse to come to the United States and was currently chef at the Fifth Floor in San Francisco); Scott Conant of New

York's L'Impero was on kettle drums made of giant pots, using wooden spoons as sticks. Fronting the band, Suzanne Goin of L.A.'s Lucques was made up in deep goth, singing into a microphone made out of a whisk. Above it all was Eric Ripert of Le Bernardin, shaking an equally inventive "tambourine" above his head and seeming to leap straight off the cover.

Truman took one look and predicted it would be a newsstand disaster. "Run it anyway," he said. "It's worth doing." It was October 2003, and chefs were becoming major celebrities, complete with screaming groupies. "You'll be glad you did," he said. "You're the first to illustrate this trend."

He was right on all counts: The cover didn't sell, but it was a watershed moment. It did not look like any epicurean publication of the past. And it was only the beginning.

"The thing about Richard," Zanne remarked at the end of his first week, "is that everyone on staff—male and female—wants to sleep with him."

I looked at that elegant woman, delighting once again in her bawdy sense of humor, thinking it was absolutely true. Richard wasn't flirtatious, but we all tumbled headlong into love with him. I think it was because he had a way of listening intently to every idea—and then making it better.

Most epicurean magazines employ stylists, whose mission is making food look pretty. Richard turned that on its head. Before the cooks diced their first onion, he weighed in on shape and color. "All the other magazines," one photographer confided, "keep asking why my shots look so much better in *Gourmet*. I tell them it's the Ferretti factor."

We'd been planning an issue on movies and food, but Richard instantly raised the ante. "Close your eyes," he commanded, walking into my office, "open your mouth, and let your imagination run wild."

He fed me a chocolate concoction. At first all I experienced was rich cream and soft butter, then chocolate came surging to the fore, followed by a little trill of cognac and the faintest bitter tinge of coffee. As the carousel of flavors whirled through my brain, I dreamed myself into a painting by Renoir. I was in a Paris restaurant at the turn of the century, gazing into an ornate gilt-edged mirror. Champagne flowed and a band played soft music as a dessert cart, laden with tartes and bombes, approached. On top sat the pièce de résistance. My eyes flew open. "It's a classic gâteau opéra!"

"You said you wanted a beautiful menu," he said, "so I thought about shooting a romantic little love story based on *Gigi*." He hummed a few bars of "The Night They Invented Champagne." "I've been going through the movie frame by frame; it could be gorgeous."

"What else is on the menu?"

"Zanne and Kempy say it's been a long time since *Gourmet* did an elegant French meal. They're thinking roast quail, perhaps with figs, in a voluptuous red wine sauce. Those beautiful eggs, for starters, scrambled with cream, spooned back into the shell, and topped with heaps of caviar. A leafy little salad in a champagne vinaigrette. Camembert so ripe it drips. Great old burgundies."

"But it's so complicated! Tell me honestly how long it took the cooks to concoct that gâteau."

"Four hours."

"Exactly! The readers always say they appreciate a challenge. Then they complain that our recipes take too much time."

"It could be fantastic. . . ." He didn't try to hide his disappointment.

"Okay," I conceded, "we'll go with the *Gigi* menu. But only if the other menu is really casual and extremely easy." I began thinking out loud. "All-American, maybe, with ingredients sourced from the supermarket. Maybe a menu from a fifties Western or something like that."

"I have another idea," he said. "Let's not shoot a second film meal. So predictable. What if we focus on the audience instead of the film?"

"But all people ever eat at the movies are candy and popcorn."

"You don't have to go to a theater to watch a movie. What if they were at home, in front of the TV? We could have them in the dark, plates on their laps. Has *Gourmet* ever done anything like that?"

"Of course not."

"Then it's perfect."

"I'm thinking chili and salad," said Gina Marie Miraglia Eriquez when Zanne assigned her to the story. Gina Marie was a voluptuous Bensonhurst beauty, with long dark ringlets and a down-to-earth air. Her entire extended family lived within a few blocks of one another, and we listened enviously as she told about the meals her mother made. A dozen people—even the parish priest—sat down to Sunday dinners of homemade lasagna, marinated eggplant, beef braciole. . . . It seemed like a charmed existence, something out of the past.

But Richard wasn't interested in chili. "We can't have people with bowls on their laps; it's too hard to see the food. Besides, where would they put the salad? They'd be juggling plates, and it would be awkward. We need an entire meal that can fit on one plate."

"Sloppy joes?" she suggested. "On biscuits?"

"Better." Richard closed his eyes, picturing it. "But won't the salad dressing make the biscuits soggy?"

"It doesn't have to be salad. I'll come up with another vegetable." She stood to go. "But I have this idea for dessert: I want it to be like one of those candy bars you buy at a movie concession. You know, chocolate and peanuts."

"Topped with popcorn?" I suggested.

"Too obvious," said Richard.

FIRST TASTE

Gina Marie removed a tray of hot biscuits from the oven, and the scent of butter soared deliciously into the air. Steam rose as she split a biscuit and ladled a thick, savory stew over the top. The scent attracted a herd of cooks, who came galloping toward us, forks in hand.

Zanne swooped in for a bite. "Is there ketchup in here?" she asked suspiciously. "I swear I taste ketchup."

Gina Marie rolled her eyes. "They're sloppy joes," she said. "Of *course* there's ketchup."

Zanne took another taste. "Kind of ordinary if you ask me. It's not very *Gourmet.*"

"Maybe you should ramp up the vinegar," suggested Kempy. "And add a little cumin."

"That's what you always say." I couldn't help myself. "Personally, I'd try a little lemon peel in the biscuits."

"And that," said Kempy, "is what *you* always say."

Richard said nothing; he was staring intently at the stew. "It's too dark," he said. "Could you use turkey instead of beef? I think it would photograph better."

SECOND TASTE

Richard smiled down at the new sloppy joes. "They look *so* much better with turkey."

Zanne reached out a fork. "Taste better too. Cleaner. But that cumin's got to go."

"I only put it in for Kempy," said Gina Marie. "It's not right. You know it's not right. Can I please take it out now?"

"Okay." Kempy was gracious in defeat.

"I'm still not sure about the ketchup," Zanne mused, "but can we talk about the biscuits? They're just not floating my boat. Can't you do better?"

"You said to make them easy." There was a slight edge to Gina Marie's voice. "So I went with buttermilk drop biscuits. They're no work at all."

"Still . . ." said Zanne. "Maybe you could try adding a little cheddar?"

"And Parmesan too," Kempy weighed in. "It would add complexity."

"While you're adding ingredients," Richard tossed in, "could you throw in some chopped parsley or scallions? Think how pretty those biscuits would be if they were lightly flecked with green. The camera would love them."

"Anything else?" asked Gina Marie.

THIRD TASTE

The sloppy-joe filling, we all agreed, was now perfect. Richard's scallions were a hit. But Zanne still had doubts about the biscuits. "I'm wondering if they really need to bake in a four-hundred-fifty-degree oven. Try them at four hundred and see how that works."

Gina Marie muttered something under her breath.

"And those green beans . . ." added Richard.

"What's wrong with my beans?" Gina Marie bristled. "They're crisp. They're perfectly seasoned. I don't see a problem."

"But look at them! Sad green things lying limply on the plate." We all stared at the plate; the beans did seem rather pitiful. "The readers need to be able to taste these meals with their eyes," said

Richard, "and if they can't see the onions, they can't imagine the flavor."

"And how"—Gina Marie's hands were now on her hips—"would you propose I make those onions pop?"

"Red onions, maybe, instead of white?" Richard was quietly reminding us all that he was a wonderful cook. "Cut larger?"

"You could quarter and then roast them," Kempy offered.

Gina Marie picked up the plate, rotating it as she gazed at the beans. "I'll quarter small red onions, drizzle them with olive oil and balsamic vinegar, and zap them in a really hot oven. Then I can toss them with the parboiled beans at the last minute. They'll look great."

"And could you leave the beans whole?" Richard suggested. "It would be such a great visual."

FOURTH TASTE

A daily diet of sloppy joes leaves something to be desired. Today when Gina Marie made up the plate, she shoved it aggressively onto the counter. "The beans are really good"—her voice held a challenge—"but I liked the biscuits better the last time around."

"It was worth a try," Zanne said a bit defensively. "But you're right. Let's go back to the last biscuits."

FIFTH TASTE

"I don't think I can do any better." Gina Marie set the entire menu before us. "The biscuits are perfect. The sloppy joes look good. And the beans are great."

"The readers are going to love it," I said.

"And I," said Gina Marie as she untied her apron, "am never eating a sloppy joe again."

On first arriving at *Gourmet,* I'd thought this intense and tortured process too hard, too time-consuming, and too expensive, but I'd been reluctant to interfere; it was not, I thought, my place to tell Zanne how to run her department. But I soon changed my mind about the testing. The *Gourmet* method was fussy and democratic, but it was an essential piece of the magazine's success. You could trust those recipes; they really worked.

But Richard took another step: He made you long to cook those dishes, and not by simply romancing the food. For this shoot Richard hired a group of models, sat them in front of a television, put on a horror film, and asked them to react to what was on the screen. You couldn't see what they were watching, but the scene was so vivid, their reactions so strong, that you yearned to be there with them. You couldn't be, of course, so you did the next best thing: You made the meal that they were eating.

You can make these biscuits larger if you're going to use them as a base for sloppy joes, but I like to make small ones to serve with barbecue, chili, fried chicken—they're extremely fast and easy and they go with just about anything.

GINA MARIE'S CHEDDAR SCALLION BISCUITS

(Adapted from *Gourmet* magazine)

• • •

6 ounces cheddar cheese

3 tablespoons Parmesan
   (finely grated)

3 scallions

¾ stick (6 tablespoons)
   unsalted butter

1¾ cups all-purpose flour

¾ cup stone-ground
   cornmeal (not coarse)

4 teaspoons baking powder

1 teaspoon sugar

1 teaspoon baking soda

½ teaspoon salt

1 cup buttermilk (well shaken)

Preheat the oven to 450 degrees.

Butter a large baking sheet.

Coarsely grate the cheddar; you should have about a cup and a half. Mix in the grated Parmesan.

Chop the scallions—both the white and the green parts.

Cut the cold butter into ½-inch cubes.

Mix the dry ingredients in a bowl, then cut in the butter with two knives until it's about the size of peas. Stir in the cheese and the scallions and then gently mix in the buttermilk, just until the dough comes together.

Drop the dough onto the baking sheet in twelve mounds, leaving space between them. Bake until fragrant and golden, about 15 minutes.

* * *

GINA MARIE'S NEXT BIG ASSIGNMENT was a children's birthday party. "I've had this idea for the cake. . . ." In her Bensonhurst accent, the word "idea" ended in "r." "What if I made little tiny cupcakes and used them like decorations? They're the perfect size; the kids could just pull them off." She mimed a toddler holding up a miniature cupcake. "They'd like that. Then when all the cupcakes are gone, the parents can eat the cake. Kind of like, you know, having your cake and eating it too."

Gina Marie iced the cake in white and covered it with jaunty polka dots. She piled the tiny cupcakes, each a vivid bright color, into a pyramid on top. Richard took one look and put the cake on the cover, setting it against a vibrant green background. It was bright, it was cheerful, it was innocence personified. And it really caught your eye.

The issue sold extremely well, so the first angry letters took us all by surprise. How dare we, subscribers wanted to know, put cupcakes on the cover? I was baffled. What were they so upset about? But as the letters continued to pour in, I began to understand that longtime readers of the magazine had decoded a message we hadn't even known we were sending.

Throughout human history, food trends have come from the top, slowly working their way down from royal tables to the modest homes of the hoi polloi. Restaurants owe their very existence to the French Revolution, which sent chefs who'd been feeding the aristocracy looking for new ways to earn money. Old-guard gourmets considered this trickle-down cuisine the natural order.

But the world of food was in turmoil. For the first time in history, food trends began to work their way up from the street. In 2004, when David Chang opened Momofuku, a tiny ten-seat restaurant in a scruffy downtown neighborhood created a national ramen craze. Then tacos took off, and street-cart cuisine began elbowing its way into white-tablecloth restaurants. The clientele for upscale restaurants was changing too; now the people who mattered most weren't old white men in suits but diverse young people in jeans, and their notion of fine dining differed enormously from that of their elders. They had no use for stuffy restaurants; they wanted noise, color, excitement.

Gina Marie's cupcakes perfectly captured this moment in time. What were cupcakes, after all, but the direct descendants of Hostess and Sno Balls? People who rejoiced in finding soufflés and croquembouches on the cover of their favorite magazine did not appreciate the apotheosis of less prestigious dishes. "What will you put on your cover next?" one reader wrote. "Hot dogs?"

They sent us vitriolic letters, using words like "gross," "distasteful," and "low." One woman insisted the cover was so offensive that she'd been forced to tear it off and throw it away. "I just couldn't bear to look at it," she wrote. Younger readers joined the battle, gleefully supporting the cake by sending in photos of their homemade versions.

The battle raged for more than a year, and while I'll admit I stirred the pot and printed the letters, I never really understood what the fuss was all about. Now, looking back, it is very clear. *Gourmet* cried, "Let them eat cupcakes!" and our readers got the message. The exclusive little world of food was growing both larger and more inclusive, and those who'd thought they'd owned it didn't like it one bit.

21

SETTING THE
RECORD STRAIGHT

"LOVE, LOVE, LOVE THE CONTROVERSY OVER THE COVER," SAID the voice on the phone. "Oh, honey, good for you!"

"Stevie!" Like many other people, I was always delighted to hear from my mother's oldest friend.

My father called him the Thin Man because he looked like Noël Coward and was the most sophisticated person any of us had ever met. Stevie Kaufmann went everywhere, knew everyone, and lived a life straight out of a thirties movie. He was the uncle I never had, the nearest thing to a living relative in New York City, and whenever he said, "Meet me for lunch," I put on my coat and walked out the door.

I found him at his regular table at Michael's, the restaurant New York media moguls preferred for power lunches. Stevie always acted like he owned the place, nodding graciously to acquaintances around the room. His table was strategically placed so that everyone who entered the restaurant had to pass by him.

Even at ninety, Stevie was the most elegant person in the room, his great dome of a head gleaming as he smiled at the parade of people, enjoying every minute. But, then, no one ever had a greater talent for finding pleasure everywhere he went.

Stevie and Mom grew up together—their mothers were best friends—and they had an unshakable ritual: Every year, Stevie took Mom to the 21 Club for her birthday. She always went—even when she was deeply depressed—because no one ever said no to Stevie.

"You should see the way they treat him!" she'd say afterward, launching into her favorite tale. "Did I ever tell you about the time Stevie showed up at 21 in his uniform? It was during World War Two, when the restaurant had a strict no-uniform policy, but they changed it on the spot. They didn't want to turn Stevie away."

She repeated this story every year, as if we'd never heard it before. Then she'd tell us all the delicious stories Stevie had told her about his famous friends. He knew Greta Garbo, Lena Horne, Rock Hudson, the brother of the king of Sweden. . . . Stevie had inherited some money at twenty-five, quit his job, and devoted the rest of his life to art, music, theater, and people. "His best friend," Mom always told us, "is Bill Blass. I think they might have been lovers, and I know they talk to each other every day."

Sometime in the early eighties Stevie announced, a little mournfully, "Blass says I need to get a job." Stevie was seventy—an almost unimaginable age to my thirty-something self—and I peered at him in disbelief. "You can't start working now," I said ungraciously. "You're much too old!"

Stevie was not offended. "I know." He shook his head ruefully. "I never intended to let this happen. My parents both died in their sixties, and I figured I would too. I thought there'd always be enough."

He went to work for the company that manufactured Bill Blass suits. I never was entirely clear what the job was; I imagine it was

mostly looking good, being charming, and taking people out to lunch, all the things Stevie was good at. Maybe it was more than that, but he never discussed it; his life was much too full to waste time talking about work.

I barely heard from Stevie during the years I was in California, so it was a surprise to pick up the phone in my L.A. office and find him on the other end. "They tell me," he said, "they've offered you the *Times* restaurant-critic post."

"How could you possibly know that?" I cried. "I just got off the phone with them."

"Don't you know I hear everything?" I pictured him on the other end of the phone, dressed in one of his gorgeous suits, airily waving a hand. "You *must* come. It's high time *you* took *me* to lunch."

I did, and often. No one was ever better company; during my six years at the *Times* we shared a lot of lunches. Once, to his enduring delight, I wrote him into a review. And, of course, Stevie was the first to call when Condé Nast came knocking. "You have to do it," he said, "if only for Mim. Think how your mother would have loved this!"

"But who told you?" I asked. Mere hours had passed since my meeting with Si.

"Oh," he said vaguely, "I used to know Si's mother, Mitzi." She'd been dead for years, but this was clearly the only explanation I was ever going to get.

Now that I was at Condé Nast, Stevie thought it was time I attended Fashion Week. "I'll get you a ticket," he said, "and you can finally meet Blass."

"Next year," I said. And I kept saying it . . . until it was too late.

"Aren't you sorry?" Stevie asked the next time we had lunch.

"Now you'll never have the chance." It was the first time in my whole life I'd seen Stevie looking sad. "Every morning I pick up the phone to call Blass. And then I remember that he's gone. I'm dreading Thanksgiving. We always spent it at his house."

When he grew uncharacteristically quiet, I tentatively suggested he might want to share Thanksgiving with us. He didn't say anything, and I blushed; of course Stevie didn't want to come to our house. He undoubtedly had dozens of more interesting invitations.

The silence lasted a few seconds and then Stevie blurted out, "Blass could have left me more in his will." It was so unlike him that I chalked it up to mourning. "It all went to some dog organization," he continued, "and he knew I could have used the money."

But today Stevie was his normal ebullient self, and I settled in to enjoy the show. "You order for me," he said to the maître d'. "You know exactly what I like." Meals with Stevie always reminded me of that scene in *Gigi* where Aunt Alicia shows the young girl how to judge jewels, eat ortolans, and choose cigars: It was a window onto a life of a bygone era. Sure enough, the waiter was soon shaving great fat slices of truffle over our pasta, the scent hovering deliciously above the table.

Stevie waited until we were alone. Then he picked up his fork and waved it at me. "I need to tell you something. I want to set the record straight."

About what? I wondered.

"They're closing my company. The owner's decided to move to Israel."

"It's probably time," I said. "You are, after all, ninety."

"Probably," he agreed cheerfully. "But the bookkeeper called the other day to ask where she should send my weekly check."

"I don't understand."

"Neither did I. But it turns out that for the last twenty years Blass was secretly paying my salary. He even left a stash so it would continue after his death. Isn't that wonderful?"

I stared at him, speechless.

"I wanted to tell you because I was so ungracious about his will." He peered at me. "Ruthie, are you crying?"

"Of course not." I hastily wiped my eyes. It wasn't the money—which would have been nothing to Bill Blass. It was the trouble he'd taken to save Stevie's pride.

When Stevie died, just short of his ninety-first birthday, the *Times* titled his obituary "The Death of an Unknown Man Who Knew Everyone." "He never did a single thing of note in his life," the author wrote, "except find a million ways to enjoy it."

The extraordinarily long obituary ran in the style section, and people talked about it for days. Stevie would have loved that. He would have loved everything about the piece, especially the notion that his talent for happiness was both worthwhile and exceedingly rare.

But I couldn't stop thinking about Bill Blass. I thought back to that first night with Giulio, when he'd looked at three chefs talking together. "You don't get it, do you?" he'd said. "What an amazing world you live in."

Now, for the first time, I thought that maybe he was the one who hadn't gotten it right. Every world has its extraordinary side. It's just that so few of us know how to find it.

22

D F W

LET ME SAY RIGHT NOW THAT IF I HAD KNOWN THAT PEOPLE FOR the Ethical Treatment of Animals had been targeting the Maine Lobster Festival for some ten years, I would have realized that sending David Foster Wallace off to write about it was a bad idea. But as the great man set off for Maine, I remained blissfully ignorant.

DFW was a legend, a brilliant, iconoclastic writer with a devoted following. I loved his work, and even though *Gourmet* had a long history of publishing great literary writers, when Jocelyn Zuckerman suggested asking him to write for us, I doubted that he'd do it. In the early years, distinguished writers Ray Bradbury, Hilaire Belloc, Kay Boyle, Annie Proulx, Joseph Wechsberg, Anthony West, Anita Loos, Anthony Burgess, Mary Cantwell, and Laurie Colwin had all appeared in *Gourmet*'s pages. In recent years we'd persuaded Pat Conroy, Calvin Trillin, Diane Johnson, Michael Lewis, Richard Ford, Julian Barnes, Jane Smiley, and, of course, Ann Patchett to write for us, but I still didn't think DFW would be game.

To be honest, I'm not sure why he agreed to do it: From the beginning he made it clear he had no interest in free trips or luxury junkets. First he turned down an all-expenses-paid voyage to a boozy gathering of malt lovers in Scotland. He scoffed at our offer to explore *la dolce vita* in Rome. The Oxford Symposium on Food held no appeal for him. We came up with dozens of suggestions; David Foster Wallace always said no.

Then Jocelyn suggested sending him to the Maine Lobster Festival. I was skeptical. "Can you see DFW at a place whose official theme is 'Lighthouses, Laughter, and Lobster'? Not exactly up his alley."

"I read somewhere that his mother's from Maine," Jocelyn persisted.

"Worth a try," I said. "But he's sure to turn us down again."

Getting DFW to say yes was only the first hurdle. On day one Jocelyn reported, "The airline lost his luggage. And he's not happy about it." Still, we had no idea how many hurdles lay ahead.

Wallace took to calling late at night, leaving long, rambling messages on Jocelyn's answering machine. "Do you think he calls then so he doesn't have to speak with a living person?" I inquired.

"Probably. But I love getting his messages. They're hilarious. I can't wait to read the piece."

Everyone in the office knew when the article arrived, because Jocelyn's laughter echoed down the hall. Still, when she came into my office clutching the hefty manuscript, her voice was not exactly filled with laughter and lighthouses.

"It's here!" She handed me the pile of paper.

"Were we expecting ten thousand words?" The manuscript was even heavier than it looked.

"It's DFW." Jocelyn's voice was oddly flat, as if she was trying to camouflage her emotions. She was, I thought, probably unaware that we'd all heard her laughter. "He does what he does." It was clear, from her demeanor, that something was wrong with the piece. She pointed at the pages. "You'd better read it for yourself."

Perusing the first page, I began to laugh; at his best David Foster Wallace is wonderfully funny, and this was a gem. He began by offering up the tangled history of Maine and lobsters. He discussed hard-shell lobsters and soft ones, noting that the festival was prepared to offer you a lobster dinner for little more than a meal at McDonald's. There was one snarky aside in which he opined that the editor of another epicurean magazine, who'd labeled this "one of the best food-themed festivals in the world," might not have spent much time sampling its delights, but he glided gracefully on to note that because lobsters are still living when they go into the pot, they are the freshest food there is.

Here he paused to consider a question. "Is it all right," he asked, "to boil a sentient creature alive just for our gustatory pleasure?" Soon he was delving into the science of pain and the ethics of death, an unstoppable torrent of words that went on for pages. At one point he referenced the infamous Nazi doctor Josef Mengele. At another he noted, "It appears to me unlikely that many readers of *Gourmet* wish to . . . be queried about the morality of their eating habits in the pages of a culinary monthly."

"Thanks," I muttered, as Wallace proceeded to question said morality for a few thousand more words, moving from lobsters to the entire animal kingdom. Would future men, he wondered, someday look back at our eating habits in much the same way we view ancient Aztec sacrifices? He ended by asking this: "After all, isn't being extra aware and attentive and thoughtful about one's food and its overall context part of what distinguishes a real gourmet? Or is all the gourmet's extra attention and sensibility just supposed to be aesthetic, gustatory?"

It was masterfully done, and for a long moment I sat at my desk, looking down at the pages with admiration and loathing. DFW had seen the mantra I'd been mouthing and raised me. He'd appropriated what was once a cute Annie Hall moment and turned it into an exercise in bioethics; nobody who read the piece could ever casually toss a live lobster into a pot again. But this was not just about lobsters; DFW was demanding that each reader examine his conscience and consider the ethics of eating.

How many people were going to take this kindly? Not many, I imagined; most were going to find it offensive. Thousands would cancel their subscriptions, and I would lose my job. It would be foolish to print this. But how could I not? I looked down at that brilliant, difficult article, wishing I had never heard of David Foster Wallace.

"You can't possibly print this piece!" Doc marched into my office, waving the pages in my face.

"I know it's edgy. . . ." I began.

Doc, normally a mild man, stamped his foot. "I don't give a damn about that," he said. "This is writing of the highest order, and it tackles real issues. But David Foster Wallace is so pretentious and arrogant, and . . ." Spluttering, he began reading some of the article out loud. "Listen to how condescending he is toward all the people at the Lobster Festival. It's insulting! You've got to get him to take some of that out. Otherwise I don't think we can print it."

Caught up in the ethical argument, I'd skipped right past the condescension, but he did have a point. "I'll see what I can do," I promised.

A few hours later I passed the art department and saw Richard and Doc nose to nose, gesticulating wildly. They rarely disagreed and I edged in to hear what they were saying. "You're serious?" Doc was almost shouting. "You really like this lobster piece?"

I slowed down, eager to hear what Richard would say. "I think it's amazing! It's the coolest thing we've ever published." All around him, the art people nodded their heads.

Larry uncharacteristically reserved judgment. "So what do you think?" I pressed him.

He was quiet for a moment. "It's problematic," he said. "Readers are going to hate it. But there's not another food magazine that would even consider running this, and it really sets us apart. But . . ."

I waited, worried about what was coming next. "I think we have to show it to Giulio. He can't sugarcoat it when he tries to sell an advertiser in. They need to know what they're getting."

"Then show it to him," I said. Was I hoping, in my secret heart, that Giulio would tell me I couldn't run this impossible piece?

Half an hour later, Giulio came bounding down the hall and I prepared for the worst.

"Is she in?" I heard him ask Robin. I looked up, apprehensive.

"This is so exciting!" He held out the pages.

"So you think you can sell someone into the piece?"

"Oh, absolutely!" His confidence surprised me. "Most of our advertising partners are on board with the evolution of the book. They understand that *Gourmet* is redefining what it means to be an authority on food. This just takes it to a new level."

"But do the readers understand that?" muttered Doc when I told him.

WALLACE HIMSELF WAS THORNY AND, when we asked for changes, irate. Passing Jocelyn's office one morning, I came screeching to a halt as I heard her say, "Have you thought about it? That colon seems very aggressive to me!"

"Are you really having a battle over punctuation?" I asked when she put the phone down.

"He's a grammar nerd," she replied. "He's very granular about the piece and he's arguing over every comma. I think his attitude is that he'll do what he does and we can take it or leave it."

"Let him have all the colons and commas he wants," I said. He'd been gracious about Doc's objections and removed the more caustic remarks about festival attendees. "But there are two more things that have to go. The Mengele reference is over the top. And I won't be a shill for PETA."

She sighed. "He won't like it. And he's upset about the title. He thinks 'To Die For' is too flip."

"So does he have a better idea?"

"No," she said, "but I do. What if we call it 'Consider the Lobster'? You know, after the M.F.K. Fisher piece."

"It's perfect!" I said. "But he'll probably hate that too."

As press time came closer, Jocelyn and DFW were still fighting it out. "The good news," she said, "is that he loves 'Consider the Lobster'; it turns out his mother is a Fisher fan. And he's reluctantly agreed to remove the reference to Mengele. But . . ."

I had a bad feeling about what was coming. "He won't budge on PETA. We've hit a wall. If you really want him to take that out, you're going to have to talk to him yourself."

I paced up and down my office, wondering what I could possibly say to persuade him. He held the trump card; he could always take his article elsewhere. This was a brilliant piece of writing, and I had no doubt the editors of *The New Yorker* or *Harper's* or *The Atlantic Monthly* would be thrilled to get their hands on it. For them it would present no problems. . . .

That's it! I suddenly realized. That's the winning argument.

I dialed his number. "I won't publish this with the reference to

PETA as it stands. And if you don't want to change it, you can surely sell it somewhere else. But you don't want to do that." I sounded a great deal more confident than I felt. "You didn't write this for a bunch of effete intellectuals for whom the whole thing is hypothetical. You wrote this for cooks. You're hoping that no cook will ever blithely throw a lobster into a pot without pondering the morality of his action. Isn't that true?"

There was a long silence.

"Yes," he said at last.

I hung up feeling victorious. Later, however, lying in bed, I thought how much easier it would have been if I'd lost the battle. This was by far the edgiest article we'd ever published, and if he'd pulled it I would have had an honorable out. I fell asleep to dream about angry subscribers descending on my office to chase me from the building and woke to the certain knowledge that I was about to lose my job. Giulio might be right: Our advertisers might be ready for articles like this one. But I was not so sure our readers were.

The night the magazine went to press, I was so jittery I couldn't cook. Michael was out of town, working on a documentary about the heroin epidemic, so I took Nick out to eat.

"Let's go to Honmura An." It was the calmest restaurant I could think of, a spare, elegant space, soothing as a spa.

Walking in the door, I thought about our first visit to the restaurant ten years earlier; I'd carried Nick up the stairs. Now he towered over me. At fifteen he was almost six feet tall, with an appetite to match. He watched me order seaweed and soba, and then he asked the waitress for shrimp tempura, chicken meatballs, and a big bowl of udon with sliced duck.

"I love these shrimp," he said as the waitress set the plate before him. The giant creatures, larger than any I'd ever seen, were flown in specially from Japan, and as Nick picked one up, a wave of nausea bubbled through me.

"Mom!" Nick looked frightened. "Are you all right?"

I waved my hands, took a few deep breaths, trying to quell the feeling. The shrimp looked just like baby lobsters. "I'm fine."

"Are you going to faint? You've gone completely white. Drink this." He handed me his glass of water.

I took a sip, concentrating on the sensation of the cold liquid sliding down my throat. I took another and felt the blood return to my head.

"What's going on?" Nick picked up a shrimp. I looked away.

"Have you ever heard of David Foster Wallace?"

"The *Infinite Jest* guy? He's Zack's favorite writer."

"We're running an article of his."

"Wow. Cool!"

"That's what I thought. I was excited he was writing for us. And then I got the article."

Nick picked up another enormous shrimp. "What's wrong with it?"

"The readers are going to hate it."

"Why?" He took a bite; the batter crackled loudly as it shattered.

I hesitated; was it fair to bring up the ethics of eating at this precise moment?

"Why?" Nick repeated, taking another shattering bite.

"We sent him to a lobster festival. . . ."

"That doesn't sound very hateful."

"As he stands there watching lobsters going into the boiling water, he starts to wonder what they feel. Does it hurt? Can they feel pain? The next thing you know he's asking whether we have the right to kill animals just because we happen to like the way they taste. In the end it comes down to whose life matters most." I pointed at my pristine seaweed. "After all, we don't *need* meat. It's perfectly possible to stay alive without killing other creatures."

"But don't you think cooks *should* be asking themselves those questions?" Nick had stopped eating, and as he stared down at the shrimp I knew he was imagining a sleek animal gliding gracefully through a turquoise sea.

"Uncomfortable, isn't it?" I said.

"Yeah. But I *want* to be aware of those things!" He spoke with so much heat that I remembered how it felt to be a teenager filled with ferocious passion. "Don't you think one of the problems of the way we live is that we're disconnected from the whole life cycle?" He stared earnestly at me before asking, "Do you want to know what I really think?"

I had the awful feeling I was about to get one of those stinging assessments your children are uniquely equipped to deliver.

"I think you're underestimating your readers. Give them some credit."

It was 2004—and that article changed everything. Two people canceled their subscriptions, but hundreds wrote in to say how much they valued a magazine that published such thought-provoking articles. "Keep it up" was the basic message.

And we did. It was DFW who gave me the courage to publish "Some Pig," David Rakoff's extremely controversial piece on the tortured relationship between Jews and bacon. Would I have dared, before DFW, to publish "The Taste of Home," Junot Díaz's essay about how his love for Asian food is inextricably linked with his yearning for his absent father? Probably not. And I'm pretty sure that before DFW I would have run, fast, in the other direction when I read Chimamanda Ngozi Adichie's "Too Hot to Handle," a feminist food piece about growing up in Africa. Every one of these articles took food writing into a deeply personal, psychological direction, and every one of them was edgy and uncomfortable. But DFW had proved that our readers appreciated a challenge, and we were all eager to stretch the traditional boundaries of food writing.

I'll admit that on first reading I was frightened of Nina Teicholz's deeply troubling investigation into the food industry's thirty-year attempt to sabotage a scientist who'd discovered a link between trans fats and cancer. "These two guys from the Institute of Shortening and Edible Oils—the trans fat lobby, basically—visited me," the scientist recalled, "and, boy, were they angry. They said they'd been keeping a careful watch to prevent articles like mine from coming out in the literature and didn't know how this horse had gotten out of the barn."

Great story. Also problematic. Procter & Gamble, the company that held the first patent for trans fats, was one of Condé Nast's biggest advertisers. I remembered Florio talking about Si's fury when a fashion editor angered a major advertiser. Would he fire me for this? We called Nina's story "Heart Breaker" and waited to see what would happen. (We never heard a word from P&G.)

And when Barry Estabrook said he wanted to go to Florida to investigate the plight of tomato pickers, once again I thought of DFW. The cut line on "The Price of Tomatoes" went like this: "If you have eaten a tomato this winter, chances are very good that it was picked by a person who lives in virtual slavery."

I had nightmares about every one of those pieces. But in those sleepless nights while we were editing the David Foster Wallace piece, I'd learned an important lesson: When something frightens me, it is definitely worth doing.

23

MENE, MENE

NO TRUMPETS SOUNDED. NO ALARMS BLARED. THE BLAND PIECE OF paper sailed onto our desks disguised as a routine memo: Florio was being named vice chairman. We all knew he was being kicked upstairs, but did any of us understand that this marked the end of life as we knew it?

I certainly did not. I was like a frog in a kettle of water and this was the moment they lit the fire, turning it up so gradually I had no suspicion that *Gourmet* would soon be cooked. If you'd told me that the end was near, I wouldn't have believed you. Halcyon times still lay ahead, but even later, when the pot was being stirred, I never really felt how hot the water had become.

That memo wrenched Florio out of Si's orbit, and he faded slowly from the scene until, like the Cheshire Cat, nothing but the grin remained. As his influence evaporated, the exuberant company he'd created vanished with it, the manic energy replaced by something sterner, sturdier, and far more predictable.

"This is going to be good" is what I thought when I first met the man who stepped into the office next to Si's. Chuck Townsend projected solid reliability. With pale-blue eyes and windburned cheeks, he was an upscale version of every Elk and Shriner in the nation, and as I watched him consume a bland white-bread lunch, I thought back to the strange and ebullient Florio meals. Things would be calmer now, I thought, more sane, more sober.

I was optimistic as I watched Chuck, the commander of the New York Yacht Club, pilot us away from the casual accounting of Steve's stewardship. But I did not reckon on the cost, did not know this would mean spending endless hours attending to the business of the magazine. Meetings that had once been held twice a year became monthly affairs, and I grew depressingly familiar with the dreary tenth-floor conference rooms. Struggling with spreadsheets and financial reports, I found myself thinking wistfully back to Truman asking, "You don't suppose Anna Wintour worries about budgets, do you?"

New bean counters seemed to appear at every meeting, and they had endless questions. "Why," they wanted to know, "are you still using analog film when digital photography is less expensive?"

"Because Richard prefers the quality" was my perennial answer. It had always been good enough for Si, who wanted the best of everything for his magazines. But now he sat silently by as we went digital.

"Can't you do something?" Richard pleaded. "The resolution and dynamic range are so much better with analog film."

I shook my head; it was a done deal. "A bad omen," Larry predicted. "The next thing you know they're going to cut back on the quality of our paper."

Richard's disappointment filled me with despair. I'd always been able to protect my people; now I felt impotent, and I worried about what was coming next.

It made me think about the moment, early in my career, when I'd finally understood what set Alice Waters apart from other chefs. I'd been interviewing Mark Miller, who had left Chez Panisse to open his own restaurant, Fourth Street Grill, and when I asked about his former boss he said, "Alice has no head for business."

"What do you mean?" I asked.

"Just look at that salad she's so proud of," he replied. "First she pays half of Berkeley to tear up their lawns and plant mesclun for her. Then she sells huge heaps of it for peanuts. I bet she loses money on every single salad that she sells."

When I mentioned this to Alice, she was unconcerned. "I want everyone to taste what salad should be," she told me. "If I had my way I'd just hand everyone a bottle of olive oil and another of vinegar and take them out to a great garden and say, 'There it is, help yourselves.'"

I understood that attitude. Working at the Swallow, our communal Berkeley restaurant, I was constantly sneaking in provisions to keep the food costs down. I brought in my own herbs, spices, stocks, and homemade jams, willing to do anything to improve the food that I was cooking.

Mark didn't miss a beat. "The problem with most chefs," he said, "is that they think it's all about creativity. They don't understand that a restaurant is, first and foremost, a business."

But it gave me an idea. How much could film cost? "What if I paid for it myself?" I asked Larry.

The look he gave me said I'd lost my mind. "Do you have any idea what it costs to process film?" Then, demonstrating once again his uncanny ability to intuit my thoughts, he added, "This isn't Berkeley. Believe me, the readers won't notice and Richard will get over it. And"—he gave me a stern look—"if you're thinking of running to Truman, don't. He'll tell you the same thing."

I let it drop. But it made me wonder how Truman was feeling now that Florio had gone. Despite their mutual dislike they'd been, in some strange way, perfect partners. Si had hired a flamboyantly competitive businessman and a passionate advocate for creativity, pitted them against each other, and sat back to watch the fireworks. In the past he'd maintained a delicate balance between the two, but now his thumb was firmly on the business side of the scale. For Truman, who'd always nurtured his people, it could not be a happy situation.

It took less than a year before Robin was leaning over my desk, her face pregnant with portentous news. "James Truman just quit!" She whispered the four words as if they were too explosive to say out loud.

I jumped back, as if the shock were physical. "Are you sure?" Stupid question.

"Si's secretary just called. She said Truman strolled into Si's office this morning and told him he was leaving. Just like that! Can you imagine? I've heard he makes two million dollars a year . . . and he's walking away. Do you think there's anybody else who'd do that?"

"Probably not." Unlike others at Condé Nast, Truman seemed bored by glamour and disinterested in money.

"Oh, God." The words came tumbling out before I could stop them. "I hope he doesn't replace Truman with someone like Chuck. Have you heard who's in the running for the job?"

Robin nodded solemnly. "It's a done deal."

"Already?"

"He picked Tom Wallace."

"Oh, no!" The editor of *Condé Nast Traveler* was a nice man, a smart man, but he had none of Truman's odd, inscrutable brilliance. This did not make me feel safe.

Diana had worked with Tom, and in her blunt fashion she was

frank in her dislike. "The *Traveler* was so much fun when Harry Evans"—the magazine's founding editor—"was there." She'd said it more than once. "But all the joy went out of the job when Tom took over." Her face always grew cloudy as she recalled the experience, and she used words like "sober," "sensible," "dependable." I thought he sounded very much like Chuck.

I didn't know Tom well, but he lived in my building, and in my first week at Condé Nast he'd invited me to lunch at the Four Seasons and tried to initiate me into the mysteries of the world I'd entered.

"Si will leave you alone." He took an earnest sip of his sparkling water. Unlike many of his peers, Tom did not seem to consider lunch at the company's most glamorous canteen an opportunity to get sloshed. "He doesn't like to interfere. But I enjoy his company, and I make sure to ask him to lunch every couple of months. He's very smart about the business, and you can learn a lot from him. If you take my advice you'll spend as much time as you can with Si."

I remembered how disappointed I'd been. I'd been looking for advice on attracting great writers, but he'd wanted to talk about business. It was a far cry from any counsel Truman ever offered, and it did not bode well for the future. Farewell the fights, I thought; Tom would never stand behind Chuck's desk mocking him. And he certainly wouldn't make me bets about my covers.

Deeply depressed, I sent Truman a note to say how sad I was to see him go. His reply came bouncing back. Was I free for lunch? This was a surprise. Truman treasured restaurants and was an ardent cook who loved talking about recipes. Once he even gave me an unusual tool for chopping vegetables. "I love my alligator," he'd said, dropping it on my desk. But in the six years we worked together, we'd shared nothing more substantial than tea.

It was a raw January day, and I pulled my coat around me,

shivering slightly as we walked west on 43rd Street. "You must be the only person in the company who has the courage to quit," I said as we crossed Eighth Avenue.

"Probably. But a quote from Joseph Campbell kept going through my head. Do you know his work?"

"The comparative-mythology guy? I've read *The Hero with a Thousand Faces,* but it was a long time ago. I don't remember much."

"You should read *Myths to Live By.* The idea that's been resonating with me is his notion that we must be willing to get rid of the life we've planned so as to have the life that is waiting for us. I'm curious about what the future might hold."

"You don't have a plan? You're just going to wing it and see what happens?"

He turned his head, offering me his snaggletoothed smile. "At the moment I *do* have a plan. I want to stop at the tennis club and buy my girlfriend some lessons. Do you mind?"

Condé Nast people didn't perform minor tasks for themselves. They routinely sent minions. As I trailed Truman into the club, I thought how pleasantly prosaic this was. He would have no trouble adjusting to the real world.

Lunch was lovely, but nothing of consequence was said, and as it ended I took a deep breath. "Can I ask you something?" This was probably my last chance to get his advice.

He looked amused. "About Si?"

What else did we talk about at Condé Nast? "I know I should try to spend more time with him. A lot of editors do. But he makes me so uncomfortable that every time he asks me to lunch, I come up with an excuse."

Truman studied me frankly. "I think you're missing out," he said at last. "He has an interesting mind and he's knowledgeable on a great many subjects. But with Si things aren't personal; I don't think he operates out of friendship or loyalty. I can't tell you the number of times he's returned from lunch with someone who's supposedly in favor saying, 'You know, we really ought to fire her.' So if you want my advice, here it is. Don't try to second-guess him. And don't worry about being his friend. The way to succeed with Si is to simply make him the best magazine you possibly can."

It was, of course, exactly what I wanted to hear. But for once I was not reassured. The memory of my latest encounter with Si floated into my mind.

I'd marched proudly into his office to announce that once again I'd scored a million-dollar advance for a *Gourmet* cookbook. He gave me a glacial stare. "Why are you taking less than you got for the first book?" he demanded.

I thought he'd misheard me. "I'm not! They're paying us a million, just like last time."

Si's look was pure contempt. "Exactly! A million dollars in 2004," he enunciated every word, "is not the same as a million dollars in 2001."

My face went red and I stood like an errant schoolgirl whose dog has eaten her homework. "How much do you want?" I asked meekly.

"More," he said.

"You won't get it," our agent had insisted when I called later that day.

"Then there won't be a cookbook. Si's the one who signs the contract," I replied.

"And to my surprise," I told Truman, "the publishers blinked. They were afraid he'd simply walk away. They agreed to advance us a million and a quarter."

Truman laughed. "There's nothing new about that," he said. "It's classic Si. A few years ago he raised ad rates and Steve was apoplectic. He went storming into Si's office, saying the marketplace was resistant and we needed to lower them back to where they'd been. Si looked up and said, 'Raise the rates another ten percent.' Steve was so angry I thought he was going to explode. But it worked! What you have to understand about Si is that when it comes to business, he enjoys the game. Editorial, however, is another story; he is deeply respectful of the editorial process.'"

"Then why are you walking away?" I didn't actually ask the question; I knew the answer. Truman had obviously enjoyed his job. He'd started groundbreaking magazines, relishing the excitement of looking into the future and figuring out what was next. He'd rejoiced in every opportunity to break new ground, and if nothing had changed, he'd have no reason to leave. *Mene, mene, tekel, upharsin:* He must have seen the writing on the wall.

But where did that leave me and my merry little band? I reluctantly accepted that I had two choices. I could follow Truman out the door, or I could do my best to make my peace with this new reality.

We parted outside the restaurant and I waved goodbye, standing for a long time as Truman wended his way across the crowded sidewalk. When I could no longer see him, I turned and walked back to Condé Nast.

From now on, I thought, I'm on my own.

24

PULL UP A CHAIR

THE SCENT OF FRESH ORANGES PERFUMED THE AIR, AND BISCUITS baked in the oven. Bacon sizzled in the pan, filling the kitchen with the generous aroma of hickory smoke. The tantalizing promise of coffee and cocoa hovered in the background.

When I was a restaurant critic, forced to eat out every night, breakfast became the most important meal of the day. I rose early every morning to make omelets and pancakes, bake coffee cake, knead bread, and I never lost the habit. I found comfort in the aromas wafting through the house, a sensory alarm clock that woke my sleeping men. I loved the way they'd tumble into the kitchen, hair still wet from the shower, teasing each other as they prepared to face the day.

I looked forward to our morning meal with a hunger that had nothing to do with food. This day, however, I was on the warpath. "Listen to this!" I picked up *The New York Times* and shook it in their faces. "I've been reading about a new shop on the Upper East Side dedicated to 'children's food.'"

Michael set his coffee on the table, carefully positioning it between the orange juice and maple syrup. "What's wrong with that?"

"There's no such thing as children's food! It's a cynical modern invention. And it's sending kids the wrong message, telling them they're a separate species who couldn't possibly like whatever the grown-ups are eating."

"But most kids *don't* like the food their parents eat." Nick poured an ocean of maple syrup onto his pancakes. He was sixteen now, with the appetite to prove it.

"And whose fault is that?" I was not unaware that, behind my back, the guys were flashing each other the resigned look that appeared each time I climbed up on my soapbox. "Japanese children aren't born with an innate craving for seaweed any more than American kids arrive in this world with a native taste for hot dogs. We *learn* to eat, and for most of human history children have done that by imitating their parents. But not anymore; now we're feeding them a special menu of fried chicken nuggets and soda pop."

"I hate to break this to you, Mom . . ." Nick stopped, hesitating, knowing he was tiptoeing into difficult territory. "But when I was growing up, I *never* ate the same food as you and Dad."

"That," I said loftily, "is entirely different."

WHEN NICK WAS SMALL, MICHAEL and I would lie in bed at night, listening to the nightmare sound of the deep, unforgiving coughs tearing through his body. He was always sick, but nobody seemed to know why. When a serious infection put him in the hospital, the doctors ran a battery of tests and discovered an immune deficiency. "This is why every sniffle turns into a medical crisis," they said. They admitted it was a rare condition and they didn't know much about it, but they also had good news. "It's virtually unknown after the age of twelve. All we have to do is give him enough antibiotics to keep him alive until then."

Nick was normal in every other way. He was affectionate, athletic, and very energetic, so we kept his illness to ourselves. No active boy should be labeled "sick." But he remained a sprite of a child, wiry and small, who seemed to exist on air. He steadfastly refused to eat anything that wasn't white, and people joked about the restaurant critic with the extremely picky kid. And they laughed when I showed up at every party with an egg in my purse, just in case Nick got hungry.

"He's never eaten a fruit or vegetable," I complained to his doctor when Nick was seven. "Shouldn't I be worried?"

"No sane child," she said patiently, "ever starved himself to death. If you had to swallow antibiotics three times a day, you'd have no appetite either."

Still, I couldn't help trying. "Won't you just *taste* a snow pea?" I urged every night as I plucked vegetables from the moo goo gai pan we ordered from the Chinese takeout place down the street. It was the only dish Nick liked.

"You know I don't eat green things." Carefully scrutinizing his plate for offending signs of color, Nick reluctantly picked up a fork and took a tiny bite, consuming his dinner with excruciating slowness. And every night I'd wonder how much of this had to do with the antibiotics, and how much of it was due to my job. A family should eat together.

"Where are *you* eating tonight?" he'd ask, looking anxiously at my watch, knowing I'd soon be walking out the door. Our son made it very clear that while he had no interest in food, he'd much prefer not eating it with us.

But I've never thought children should be forced to sit quietly while the grown-ups indulge in the stately theater of fine dining, and I didn't want to inflict that on Nick. Still, I tried, at least a couple of times a week, to find a place he could enjoy, and for a person with no use for food, Nick was remarkably knowledgeable about New York restaurants.

He could tell you, for instance, how fast the dance floor at the Rainbow Room revolved and exactly how long it took to circumnavigate the room. He knew that the Palm had the city's finest hash browns and which chefs at Benihana—a bastion of white food—played the best tricks with your dinner, flipping bits of chicken high into the air.

He would tear out of the elevator at Windows on the World to press his slight frame against the huge glass windows. It was like looking down on a toy village, cars nosing silently through crowded streets while, off in the distance, planes took off and landed at faraway airports. "Being so high up makes you feel very important," he said. Which was, of course, the point.

When we went to Jekyll & Hyde—a funhouse of a place, complete with moaning walls and a band of musical skeletons—he insisted on writing the review. "This is a restaurant for kids," he argued, "and I think a kid should review it for your paper."

He approached the assignment with great seriousness, thoughtfully tasting the curly fries (too spicy), the chicken (overcooked), and the corn (mushy). "It's more like a talking playground than a restaurant," he concluded, "and not nearly as good as Hatsuhana."

But as far as Nick was concerned, nothing was as good as Hatsuhana. His love for the venerable Japanese restaurant had very little to do with the food and everything to do with Osada-san, a small, gentle sushi master with an extraordinarily kind face and an almost mystical ability to discern his customers' desires.

For years he gave me the most exotic tidbits he could conjure up—pungent fermented squid guts, shiraku (he called the delectable cod sperm "children of the clouds"), and sawagani, tiny freshwater crabs the size of a Tic Tac. For Michael, he stuck strictly to tradition—tuna, yellowtail, and fluke. Then, turning to Nick, he would bow and say, "For you, something very special," as he handed him a pristine bowl of rice.

We were relaxed at those dinners, secure in the knowledge that Osada-san would never give us anything we didn't like. Sometime around Nick's eighth birthday he dipped a brush into the sweet, inky eel sauce and swished it across Nick's rice. Surprised, Nick squinted down at the black squiggle. Then he picked up his chopsticks and took a tiny, tentative taste. Then he took another.

Osada-san beamed.

On our next visit Nick looked up innocently and said, "Do you have something else I might want to eat?"

I was stunned—and a little hurt; he'd never trusted me that much. "Of course," said Osada-san. I waited, fascinated, to see what the chef would offer up. To my deep disappointment, it was a madeleine.

It seemed like a wasted opportunity, but Osada-san was both wily and wise. The next time Nick asked for something new, he placed a morsel of eel atop the rice. Nick frowned at the burnished sliver; then he put it in his mouth.

It was just the beginning. Now, on each visit, Osada-san introduced Nick to another new food. He started with the mildest fish—tuna, scallop, shrimp—but over time the flavors grew more intense, and before long he had initiated my son into the mysteries of crisp giant clam and pungent mackerel.

Still, I was taken aback, when, on Nick's tenth birthday, Osada-san scooped up some bright-orange sea urchin roe. "I think you're ready," he said, handing it over.

Sea urchin is a love-or-hate proposition. Nick's eyes flew open in shock, and I thought the chef had finally gone too far. Then Nick's eyes closed, and a look I'd never seen before crossed his face, as if he was tasting something rare and precious, something he had never even dared imagine. "That"—he opened his eyes—"is the most delicious thing I've ever tasted."

Over Nick's head, Michael and I stared at each other. We'd both had the same thought: Maybe the illness is over.

RELEASED FROM HIS ANTIBIOTIC PRISON, Nick became a food explorer, eager to discover the unfamiliar world of flavor. Trying to make up for all the years of lost appetite, he wanted to taste everything. There was nothing he wouldn't try. Brain ravioli? Bring it on! Spicy Sichuan peppers? Yes, please. Ramps, suckling pig, tongue tacos. Once, trying to impress him, I said I'd been eating ant eggs. "Oh, those," he said disparagingly. "They don't really taste like much."

His body, grateful to be fed, shot up, and Nick morphed from a delicate child into a gangly teenager towering over everyone in his class. He reached six feet and kept on growing. He let his hair go wild, and the abundant curls added a few extra inches. A year earlier, restaurants had been asking if he wanted a booster seat; now they asked if he'd like a drink.

I could not have been happier. Michael has never been an adventurous eater, but Nick was willing to go anywhere and try anything. "Admit it," I said now. "All those years of watching us eat must have had some effect. Once you got off the antibiotics, you wanted to devour the world."

"You're probably right," he conceded. "I certainly wouldn't have touched any of those things they're selling in that kid food shop. Are you going to write about it?"

"Maybe for my next 'Letter from the Editor.'"

"I'd be happy to consult on that," he offered, "if you'll help with my English assignment." He scooped up the last of his pancakes. "My teacher wants us to do a project on the books we studied this semester. She said we can do anything—a poem, a screenplay, an ad, even a game—but she hopes we'll surprise her. She said someone always comes up with something really original; this year I want it to be me."

"What are you going to do?"

"I was thinking of a cookbook; I bet no one's ever done that."

I answered casually, trying to conceal my delight. "How would you go about that?"

"Look for food references in all the books. Then find recipes for them. Will you help?"

Michael left for Louisiana later that day, to interview a wrongfully incarcerated soldier. (Thanks to his piece, the man was ultimately released. But that's another story.) In his absence, Nick and I holed up in the apartment all weekend; while he scoured the novels for food references, I went through the cookbooks. "And now," he said, when we'd collected all the recipes, "I'm going to rewrite them."

"Rewrite them?"

"You didn't think I planned on just handing in a bunch of ordinary recipes?"

Well, yes, that's exactly what I'd thought.

"You're always saying you can learn a lot about a person by watching what they eat. I thought I'd look at recipes the same way." Nick handed me the recipe for scrapple he'd concocted for *The Great Gatsby*. Along with ordinary ingredients like pig's feet, onions, and cornmeal, he'd included a pinch of escape, a couple of teaspoons of aspiration, and a healthy handful of education. It was, I thought, brilliant.

I kept looking up recipes; he kept rewriting them, growing

increasingly inventive as the weekend wore on. The language became more playful; the instructions for Huck Finn's Stolen Fruit Salad began, "Do you dare to peel a peach?"

When we got hungry, we cooked, stir-frying Thai noodles, rolling out pasta for lasagna, baking brownies. I don't think I've ever been happier.

But I was worried; this was such a mad project. "I hope your teacher has a sense of humor," I said as he typed up the final draft. "She could give you an A. But she could just as easily flunk you."

"I know that." He ran his fingers through his hair, making it stand straight up. "But I don't really care. Doing this was so much fun—and I learned a lot. Isn't that what counts?"

"I wish you could have known your grandfather," I blurted out. "He would have loved this book. And he would have loved you."

I'd embarrassed him. When Nick did not reply, I said, "Will you read the 'Letter from the Editor' I've been writing?"

He read slowly, nodding his head. I watched as he perused the last paragraph: "The most important lesson we learn at the table is that great rewards await those who take chances. Do we really want to be telling our children, 'Just eat your nice chicken nuggets'? It would make so much more sense to say, 'Pull up a chair. Take a taste. Come join us. Life is so endlessly delicious.'"

"Nice, Mom." It was his greatest compliment. "You know, I think we kind of wrote the same thing. We just used different words."

P.S.: Nick's teacher, obviously a woman of extraordinary discernment, wrote little notes all over the paper. "Hello, Mr. Prufrock," she wrote next to the peaches. And on the front of his cookbook, she penciled an enormous A+.

25

DOT COM

IF YOU NEED INSPIRATION WHEN YOU'RE PLANNING A PARTY, chances are you'll leaf through cookbooks and magazines, dreaming up dinner. But if you come home from the farmers market with a bushel of ripe peaches or a fine cheese pumpkin, you'll probably head to the Internet.

Cooks embraced the Internet from the very start, immediately appreciating the ease of googling an ingredient and finding dozens of different ways to use it. They treasured the ability to comment on a recipe and warn other cooks away from a dud or to suggest alternative methods. Instant communities sprang up, as cooks asked and answered dozens of questions. The Internet literally transformed the way we cook.

The possibilities the Internet held for *Gourmet* were so exciting that I began fighting for a website from my first day on the job. But Si was wary of the Web; while other media companies invested in technology, he sank a reported one hundred million dollars into a new print magazine. "Sank" is the appropriate word: *Portfolio,* his flashy business magazine, flamed out after two years. Meanwhile, he pursued an Internet strategy that involved shoveling the contents of his many magazines into super-sites like Epicurious and style.com.

But having Epicurious as our only online presence made me miserable, and for years I tried to persuade Si that *Gourmet* deserved a standalone site. I presented data about recipes being the most wanted content on the Web. Si didn't care. My talk about Web advertising strategies interested him not at all. After each session I stomped back to my office to sit by, impotent and angry, as Epicurious siphoned off our recipes.

I did not fume alone. Everyone at *Gourmet* hated Epicurious. They were our archenemy. "We're getting robbed!" Zanne complained. "And what's worse is the way our recipes get tossed in with all the others as if there was no difference between us and *Parade, Self. . . .*" Morosely, she listed all the other publications whose recipes lived on Epicurious. "At least *Bon Appétit* has a test kitchen," she said darkly, "but some of the others . . ." I thought of our insane testing process and the vast amounts of money we spent ensuring that our recipes were absolutely foolproof.

When I complained to Chuck, over yet another bland lunch, he sighed deeply. "I hear the same thing from Anna Wintour," he said. "You both want to support your brands with standalone sites. I certainly understand, but Si won't budge."

I don't know what made Si change his mind, but when he finally did, he came in person to deliver the news. "I want you to create gourmet.com as quickly as possible," he said as he sat down.

In my excitement, I began to babble. "You won't be sorry; we're going to create the best food site on the Web. We've got so many ideas! We're going to hire a videographer and put webcams in the kitchen so readers can get to know the cooks; I was thinking we might even script a little show and call it *Soup Opera.* Just a few minutes from the kitchen every day. And we'll create an online course: 'Learn to Cook with *Gourmet.*'"

Was that a smile? Hard to tell. "That could be lucrative," he said cautiously.

"We'll go behind the scenes of all the restaurants we review," I rushed on, "take cameras right into the kitchens. We'll get our foreign correspondents to send daily dispatches from every corner of the world. We'll put up episodes of our television show, *Diary of a Foodie.* And then of course there's all the great content from the past. . . ."

Si's face told me I was talking too fast, that he found my enthusiasm frightening. I reined myself in, tried to slow down. "Our recipes alone should quickly build traffic; everybody knows they're the best-tested and most reliable recipes in the world."

Si fidgeted, looking more uncomfortable than usual. "No," he said.

"No?"

"You can't have your recipes."

"Excuse me?" I struggled to understand what he was saying.

"Every recipe published in *Gourmet* belongs to Epicurious. That will not change."

For a moment I was too stunned to speak. When I'd mastered my emotions I squeaked, "Are you telling me you want us to create a website *without recipes*? I'm sorry, but that's insane!"

Si drew himself up. "Epicurious," he said with regal deliberation, "is the oldest recipe site on the Web. It is very successful." He rose, ponderously, from the chair. "It will continue as in the past." He turned toward the door; the audience was over.

"Wait!" I couldn't not try. "What if we put the recipes up on both Epicurious and gourmet.com?"

"That risks cannibalizing their traffic, and we don't want to do anything to jeopardize our most successful website. When readers want recipes, we'll just redirect the traffic from *Gourmet* to Epicurious." He had reached the door now, but he turned to throw me a bone.

"Any *extra* recipes you create," he said graciously, "anything that hasn't run in the book, are yours to use as you see fit." His smile suggested I should be grateful for this gift.

"IT'S A DISASTER!" DOC WAS appalled.

"Worse than that," said Larry gloomily. "It could destroy us. Building a website and staffing it is going to cost a fortune; I've been working on the figures. How are we supposed to make it back if the recipes live on Epicurious? They'll get all the ads." He darted out of the office and returned with a handful of documents.

"Do you want to know how much we spend on creating the recipes?"

"No," I said. He didn't have to tell me that the meticulous *Gourmet* system ate up a small fortune.

Larry ignored me. "The kitchen budget is huge. Salaries for twelve cooks, three dishwashers, a photographer, and his assistant. Food costs alone run more than a hundred grand a year. Props for photographs. Corporate charges for the kitchen. Not to mention copyediting the recipes. And we're supposed to just hand them over for free?"

"Epicurious should at least share the costs," said Doc. "If the recipes are going to live on their website, it's only fair."

"It would be simple to do," Larry pointed out. "Just bookkeeping; no actual money need change hands. All they'd have to do is shift some of the costs on paper, put some of the expenses on their budget instead of ours."

But when we presented the figures to John Bellando, the chief financial officer, he laughed as if we'd told a hilarious joke. "That," he said succinctly, "is not going to happen."

"I blame myself," I said as we gloomily left the office. "I kept pushing for our own website. I never dreamed they'd handicap us like this."

"It's not your fault," said Larry. "How could you have imagined this? How could anyone? Of course we should have our own website. Food sites are huge."

"Yeah," I said glumly, "but what people want are recipes."

"We can't have a website without recipes," Larry agreed. "And unfortunately I can only think of one solution. The kitchen's going to have to create twice as many."

"That'll be great for morale," I muttered.

"Not to mention the budget," he added. We stood there, the two of us, envisioning the huge piles of food the cooks were now going to require.

Looking back, I should have just said no. But, reluctant to be a squeaky wheel, I drove on like a good girl, devoting more and more resources to a money pit that could never be solvent, a hungry maw that could never be sated, a future we could never quite reach. I knew I was tilting at windmills, but I loathe confrontation and I kept hoping that somehow it would be okay.

There were high points. We were the first print magazine to hire a full-time video producer, and through her work readers came to know—and love—all the cooks. We were able to demonstrate techniques—boning fish, icing cakes, sharpening knives. We created crazy recipes for ingredients that would never have made it into the magazine: offal, insects, corn silk, and carrot tops. Best of all, for the first time we had the luxury of space. Now, whenever someone came up with an offbeat idea, it was easy to say yes. "We can always put it on the Web. . . ." became our mantra.

And that is exactly what I said when Ian Knauer and Alan Sytsma approached me about the goat.

Ian Knauer was our most unorthodox cook. A talented chef, he was also a farmer, forager, and hunter, and this unique set of skills set him apart from everyone else in the kitchen. You never knew what he'd show up with: a deer he'd shot over the weekend, the season's first chanterelles, a slew of ramps he'd stumbled across in Prospect Park. Ian came to us as a backup recipe tester, and when I told him we were promoting him to full-time food editor, he stared at me for one shocked second and then said, "Shut the fuck up!"

Now he was poking his head into my office. "Alan and I have an idea—" he began.

Alan picked it up. "We just saw this cool documentary called *A Son's Sacrifice*—"

"Slow down," I said.

Ian gestured to Alan to continue. "It takes place in a halal butcher shop filled with live animals; you choose your beast and then they slaughter it."

"So," Ian picked up the thread, "we want to do a story about how it feels to watch an animal make the transition from living, breathing creature to something that you cook."

Five years earlier, this story would have been too gruesome to consider. Now I hesitated, wondering if *Gourmet* readers were ready for this.

"It could be very powerful," Alan pleaded. "The meat movement is starting to take off; people are really interested in butchering."

He had a point. The artisanal food movement had turned butchers into heroes, and nose-to-tail classes were selling out. Maybe this was worth doing?

"We can always put it on the Web," I said.

* * *

THEY RETURNED FROM QUEENS CARRYING two huge black plastic sacks, and you could smell them halfway across the building. The reek of the abattoir was so intense it seemed they had brought the entire contents of the butcher shop with them. The goat's body was still warm, and as they drew closer the primal scent grew stronger. By the time they reached the kitchen door, the animal funk was overwhelming. Up close, the sharp metallic smell of freshly spilled blood made the hair on the nape of my neck rise; despite my strong wish not to, I put my hand over my mouth. For a moment I stopped breathing.

"I can't believe the guards let you in." I cautiously lowered my hand.

"They didn't seem happy," Ian admitted. "But we flashed our employee passes and ran for an elevator before they could stop us. The doors were just closing."

"I hope it was empty."

Ian and Alan exchanged a glance. Ian heaved his plastic bag onto the kitchen counter. "Anna Wintour was in there."

I stared at him, fascinated and appalled. "What did she do?"

"What could she do? She just kept backing into the corner until she couldn't go any farther."

I watched as he removed sundry bits of bloody goat from the bag. "Goat tacos," he said, "are on the menu."

I eyed him suspiciously—did *Gourmet* readers want goat tacos? Briefly, I envied Anna; she didn't have to dream up ridiculous ways to generate traffic for her website.

Later, reading the story, I was ashamed of myself. There was nothing remotely ridiculous about the article Ian and Alan had written.

The halal butchers they introduced were proud men who had invested every penny they had in their shop. After September 11, they said sadly, everything changed and their once-thriving business began to struggle. Faith kept them going: They sincerely believed they had a God-given mission. Their goats were humanely raised on a rural hillside, and they were convinced their customers would appreciate how much finer they were than ordinary goats, how much more delicious. "It is this food"—the butcher spoke reverently—"that can help the rest of America accept Islam."

As Ian and Alan waded among the flock of goats, trying to select the finest animal, the butcher stood to one side, sharpening his knife. He prayed over the chosen goat, thanked him for his life, and dispatched the beast with a single slash to the throat. As he delivered the carcass into Ian's hands, he said quietly, "I know you guys will treat him well."

It was a solemn moment, for the goat represented something much bigger than food to these butchers. It was hope for the present—and a prayer for the future. Looking back, it occurs to me that it was the perfect metaphor for gourmet.com.

26

EDITOR OF THE YEAR

THE MINUTE I WALKED INTO DI PALO'S, WITH ITS FAMILIAR SCENT of salami, prosciutto, chilies, and cheese, I could feel my body begin to relax. That cheerful swirl of scent and color always makes me happy. Lou Di Palo pulled off his apron and gave me a brief hug; from behind the counter, his brother Sal and sister Theresa smiled and waved. I'd probably live longer, I thought, if I stopped in every day.

"We've known Ruthie forever." Lou released me and turned his charm on Tony Case, the *Adweek* editor who was following me around to get color for a story. "In those days she was just a neighborhood kid who liked to cook."

"I used to come here," I added, slipping into the familiar comfort of this conversation, "and stand on the endless line while Lou romanced the Mafia moms."

They were small, those women, always dressed in black, with thick stockings and sensible shoes. But at the sight of me—the only young person in the shop—they straightened up and circled around, firing off fast questions. "You like to cook?" Their fingers jabbed, their bodies rocked as they reeled off favorite recipes, desperate to share their secrets. They yearned to pass them on to the next generation, but their children didn't care for cooking. I was a last resort.

"I was standing right here when I learned to make that fresh pasta in my first cookbook," I told Tony. "And I still use the Sunday sauce another lady gave me."

"Mrs. Bergamini." Lou fished in his pocket for a small triangular knife. "What a cook!"

"And what was the name of that great baker?" I asked, remembering the small bakery around the corner he'd sent me to.

"Anna Pappalardo! I miss her bread."

It was the best bread I've ever eaten, baked in an ancient brick oven the diminutive couple had somehow carried onto the boat from Bari. Their loaves—just a few every day—were sturdy as the stones they resembled. But when you picked up a knife and sheared off a slice, a mysterious fragrance came floating out that made you think of a forest on a sunny day in fall. Each bite was like tasting history, like savoring the first loaf of bread ever baked.

Lou closed his eyes and began tapping on one of the enormous wheels in the center of the shop, working with the concentration of Michelangelo hammering into marble. It broke into two plump crescents, and golden shards tumbled onto the table. He picked one up and held it out. "Look at that! This is the fall cheese, made when the grass is ripe and the milk so rich you can taste the wildflowers in the field." He set the shard on a square of wax paper; it crinkled musically.

"Taste that! You know all Parmigiano is made only of milk, but this particular cheesemaker keeps the milk from each cow separate. After a while you learn to tell the difference."

The consummate storyteller, Lou reeled off one tale after another as the editor scribbled and the photographer snapped pictures, framing us between great blocks of cheese and hanging salamis. This, I thought, is the image Tony had been wanting: a kinder, gentler Condé Nast.

Lou removed a small white ball from the bowl on the counter and peeled open the plastic wrap. "I want you to taste our mozzarella." As he sliced into the soft orb, the cheese sent creamy liquid spurting across the counter. "See this?" Lou corralled it with his knife. "Refrigerate mozzarella and you kill it. When it gets cold the milk solids tighten, going from liquid to solid, and the cheese never recovers. It changes the taste and the texture. We make it fresh every day, from the milk of Jersey cows, and we never allow our cheese to see the inside of an icebox." He handed us each a slice and we put them on our tongues, as reverent as if he were offering us Communion. The disk was rich, round, virginal, and as the flavor reverberated through my body I thought it had been far too long since I'd worshipped at this particular altar.

Karen Danick's impeccable PR instincts had hit on the perfect way to frame the story about why *Adweek* had named me Editor of the Year for 2007: She wanted me to show Tony that I was not like the others at Condé Nast. "You think AnnaGraydon-DavidPaige spend their time shopping in Little Italy?" she asked. "You're not like them. I could hardly believe it the first time I met you! Before the interview, I had my hair blown out, a manicure, and my makeup done. Then I walk in and what do I find? You're wearing some weird jacket with apples printed all over it, your hair is a huge frizzy mess, and you don't have a drop of makeup. In fact, after I was hired the first thing Maurie said was, 'You have to get her to do something about her hair'!"

Now, riding the subway back uptown, I saw how right she'd

been: Tony had been charmed by this little outing, and we laughed all the way back to the office. But the laughter died when I saw Robin's face.

"They need you in the art department." Her voice had gone strangely flat and she was giving me a significant stare, trying to telegraph something. What? *"Richard"*—she gave the word great emphasis—"said to bring you over the *minute* you returned."

I gathered that Richard's problem was not for outside ears; he wanted me on my own. "Be right back," I said to Tony, following Robin down the hall.

The moment we were out of earshot, she put out an urgent hand. "It's not Richard; it's Tom Wallace. You're to go upstairs right away."

Adrenaline shot through me; what was wrong? Riding the elevator to the tenth floor, I tried to think what this summons might be about. *Gourmet* was coming in on budget. Newsstand sales were strong. We were racking up awards: ASMEs, Emmys, Beards. And now this *Adweek* honor. I was dutifully creating the website. What could possibly be wrong?

Tom didn't beat around the bush. "You're getting a new publisher."

"Now?" I went rigid with shock. "Giulio's leaving? Before he can capitalize on *Adweek*? Why stop the momentum when things are going so well?" I thought about the way ads went down when publishers changed; the timing was terrible.

"You know how these things work." Tom was all business. "Giulio's done an excellent job and he deserves a bigger book. Paige Rense is unhappy with her publisher, so Si's decided to move Giulio to *Architectural Digest*."

"Who's coming to *Gourmet*?"

"We haven't decided that yet."

"I guess we know who counts around here." It was foolish to

let my bitterness show, but I was too angry to care. "I really don't believe this."

Tom stared at me so coldly that I hardly recognized the nice man I'd once known. "Don't be naïve; that's the way it works," he said. "You should know that. When publishers do well they move on; I had five publishers in fifteen years at the *Traveler*. You'll be fine. What you should be concentrating on right now is the website; how are things moving on that front?"

Afraid I might say something I'd regret, I did not answer. "I have to go. The reporter from *Adweek* is waiting to finish the interview."

"Don't say anything about this," he cautioned as I left. "We haven't made the announcement, so you have to keep it to yourself. Si just wanted to make sure you were the first to know."

And he didn't have the decency to tell me himself! Things had really changed; for the first time since I'd arrived, I did not feel that Condé Nast was on my side. It was a cold, lonely feeling and I stalked down the hall, so upset my hands were shaking. I needed to calm down.

I went into the nearest bathroom and stared into the mirror; a bright red spot burned on either cheek. I turned on the tap and let the water run cold, then kept splashing it on my face, over and over, until the spots were gone.

"Crisis?" Tony looked up as I entered my office. He politely averted his eyes from the damp patches on my shirt.

"Nothing major." I could feel my smile sitting slightly askew, but he seemed not to notice. "We have to make a few adjustments. It's the nature of the beast."

"So"—he took out his pencil—"let's talk about your publisher. How do you and Giulio get along?"

* * *

WHEN THE INTERMINABLE INTERVIEW FINALLY ended, I stormed down the hall to Giulio's office.

"Why didn't you warn me?" I shouted.

He looked guilty and miserable. "They made me promise not to. And until today I wasn't sure it was going to happen."

"But how could you let this happen now?"

"Do you really think I had any choice?" He seemed genuinely chagrined. "They said it was my call, but you know it wasn't."

"C'mon, be honest, you wanted it."

He was too decent to lie. "It's a bigger book. It's a challenge. But if you move on to something else, I'll always want to do it with you. You know that. We're an awesome team."

"Not anymore."

"They're bringing in a really good guy to replace me." Always a salesman, he began his pitch. "Have they told you about Jeff?"

"What they told me is that they don't know who's going to be my next publisher."

"That's not true. A friend of mine is coming over from *Parenting*. I've known Jeff a long time; we worked together at *GQ* and I know you'll like him. He'll do a wonderful job."

"Why don't they give it to Tom Hartman? He's been your deputy from the beginning. He knows the clients, and we all love him."

"They don't think he's ready."

"They didn't think you were either." I almost said it.

I GOT BACK TO FIND Robin gnawing on her nails. "Jill Bright wants to talk to you."

I sighed. "What now?"

The head of Human Resources could sound cheerful on the grimmest occasion. Now she was positively chirpy. "We've decided to bring someone in from outside as your new publisher." She said it as if Christmas had arrived early. "We think you should meet him. When would you like to do that?"

"The sooner the better, I guess."

"He'll be there in half an hour."

Jeff Wellington was a pale version of Giulio: about the same age, nicely dressed but without the striking looks and instant charm. Still, his smile was warm and he said all the right things: He liked what we were doing; the magazine had momentum and he planned to capitalize on that. This was a fantastic opportunity and he was thrilled to be returning to Condé Nast.

"A bit bland," I told Nick and Michael, "but he seems like a good guy. The magazine's on solid ground. I hope it will be okay."

By six the next morning, when the hair and makeup people were fluffing me for another day with Tony, I had worked myself into an even more optimistic frame of mind. Giulio thought a lot of Jeff. I had liked him. Condé Nast had not abandoned *Gourmet*. It was going to be okay.

Tony and the photographer were waiting in my office, and I spent all morning cavorting for the camera. For the final shot they asked me to hop onto the low radiator in front of the floor-to-ceiling windows. "That's it!" said the photographer, squinting into the viewfinder. "The lights of Times Square are glowing behind you and the entire city's at your feet. It's perfect. We're done here. Let's break for lunch."

The moment they were gone, Giulio peered around the door. "Is the coast clear?"

He came in and carefully shut the door. Something was wrong; my door was never closed. "Has anyone called about your new publisher?"

I let out my breath. "No worries. Jeff came by last night and we talked. I liked him."

Giulio stared at me for a moment. "But nobody's spoken with you today?"

"I've been with *Adweek* all morning."

He ran his hand across his short hair, an almost desperate look in his eyes. Haltingly, he said, "I'm not supposed to tell you this, so don't let on that you know, but there's been a change of plan. They've decided that Amy and I are just going to switch jobs."

I stared at him, aghast. "Let me get this straight: Yesterday Amy was being pulled away because Paige Rense wasn't happy with her. But now they've decided that although she's not good enough for *Architectural Digest,* she'll do for *Gourmet?* Oh, that's swell."

"It is swell," he insisted. "Amy and Jeff are both friends of mine, but she's here at Condé Nast, so there's no ramp-up. She's got corporate's backing. She knows luxury. It'll be a seamless transition."

Once a salesman, I thought bitterly; he can't help himself. "You know as well as I do that if this is a promotion for you, it's a demotion for her." My anger was so sharp I could taste the bile in my throat. "They can't think much of *Gourmet.* What a great message to send our advertisers!"

"Really, Ruth," he kept saying over and over, "this is a good thing."

I did not believe that. Happily, however, I had no idea of what lay ahead. So all I said was, "Could their timing be any worse? They might as well kill the book now."

27

BEING BRAND RUTH

THE BAD THINGS HAPPENED FAST.

One minute we were on top of the world and the next ads were shrinking, newsstand sales slumping, and fear was stalking the halls of 4 Times Square. That fall *House & Garden* closed, sending rumors rioting through the building. *Portfolio* was doomed! *Men's Vogue* was toast! Layoffs loomed and huge cuts were surely coming.

We survivors danced on the edge of the volcano, unwilling to admit that anything had changed. New York began to seem like a giant publicity machine, whose main purpose was reassuring everyone that things were fine. It was the perfect moment to launch our website; people were eager to help us throw a party that made not a single concession to the new economic reality.

Karen persuaded Daniel Boulud to host the gala at Bar Boulud, which was just about to open. "Everybody wants to come!"

she exulted. "I'm turning people away right and left! And wait until you see the donations we're getting for the goodie bags!"

Gourmet had thrown many spectacular parties over the years, but this one was different. Daniel seemed to sense that an era was coming to an end, and he created a sumptuous feast that snaked down the stairs to the wine cellar, through the many subterranean kitchens, up to the bar, and across the entire restaurant. It was a spectacular edible odyssey.

The journey began in the wine room; I stopped to sample a mushroom risotto ball that crackled in my mouth, leaving a haunting earthy flavor in its wake.

In the bar, a chef stood beside an entire leg of Serrano ham, holding the delicate black hoof with one hand as he carved with the other. "These Iberian pigs stuffed themselves on acorns." As I bit into the sheer rosy slice, I imagined I could taste nuts in the soft lacy fat at the edge of the meat.

In the next room, Daniel had set out salmon in a dozen different preparations. There were also little pink shrimp in bright billows of garlic-splashed aioli and octopus smoked until the lavender flesh was smooth as velvet.

I found Doc in the adjoining kitchen, hovering over the charcuterie. "Have you tried the boudin noir?" I ate one, and a memory of blood and metal shivered through my body. "Have another," he said. "You need to fortify yourself for all the lies you'll have to tell tonight."

I moved on to another kitchen, where chefs were serving coq au vin. Doc was right, I thought, spooning up the stew and idly wondering where they'd found the old roosters that gave the dish its robust character.

"*C'est bon?*" asked Eric Ripert. We stood together, watching a chef pull fish and chips from a vat of merrily bubbling oil; setting it on a little square of paper, he showered it with salt and handed it over. Burning hot, the crisp golden batter shattered to expose the cool white sashimi-soft flesh of the fish. I held out my hand for another.

The trail wound through pâtés, foie gras, tiny game pies, and rabbit terrines, each more seductive than the last.

Upstairs the éclairs waited, long pastries bursting with pralines, chocolate, mocha. Scattered among the sweets were small scoops of grapefruit sorbet topped with white chocolate. The ice was spare and tart against the voluptuous sweetness of the chocolate, shocking you to attention. I was concentrating on the flavors when Karen began tugging at my sleeve.

"Can I borrow you for a minute?"

She dragged me off to explain to yet another columnist why it was better, so much better, that Epicurious had our recipes. "It offers us so many wonderful options!" I cried. *Gourmet* could concentrate on literature, travel, politics. "It's a win-win situation for readers," I gushed to another reporter. "Since Epicurious will have our recipes, we can devote ourselves to giving readers daily updated content on all the other topics that we cover."

"Boy, you're good." Doc stood off to one side, looking slightly bemused, as I spun these tales for the reporters. "Do you think anyone's buying it?"

"Only if they're idiots," I mumbled. But here was Karen, once again tugging at my arm.

"Can I borrow you?" Towing me toward the *Post*'s gossip columnist, she whispered gleefully, "We just caught a crasher trying to steal a coat! A very expensive one! It's going to make all the papers!"

People romped from one station to another, eating as if this were their last night on earth. As the hour grew late, the vertiginous swirl of celebrities, press, and chefs grew progressively louder. I'd promised I'd be the last to leave, but by midnight I was regretting it. I'd had too much to eat, too much to drink, and people were still flooding through the door. When I met Doc again, over the ripe Saint-Marcellin and Époisses, I groaned.

"It's a great party!" he was saying as David Chang reached around him to snag a piece of cheese.

"Doc is so fucking cool!" David said. "Who do you know who has the fucking nickname Doc? If I had a nickname I would want it to be fucking Doc. How cool is Doc? I'm fucking Doc!"

Doc smiled, looking elegant and embarrassed; a nearby reporter was taking down every word.

"You've made Karen's night," I told him. "The hottest chef in the country wants to be called Fucking Doc. That's bound to go viral."

Our newest publisher stood back, watching it all. After Giulio's departure, nobody lasted long—Amy had stayed less than two months. Tom Hartman looked exhausted. "Good thing you threw the party now," he said. "I have a feeling we won't be doing this again."

"Really?" I looked at his tired face. "Are things that bad?"

He nodded. "Nobody up in corporate wants to admit it, but we're in a recession and it's going to get a lot worse before it gets better. Especially for us."

"Why us?"

The look he gave me said I was absurdly naïve. "C'mon, Ruth. If you're Tiffany's and you have to reduce your ad spend, who are you going to keep—*Vogue* or *Gourmet*? It's a no-brainer. If you're a cruise line, are you going to cut us or the *Traveler*? And think about appliance companies. Viking makes the lion's share of its money on new buildings; what happens when the building stops? Times are tough and they're going to get tougher."

I liked Tom enormously. He'd been Giulio's number two and

he was a smart, decent man with a fine sense of humor. He had an MBA from Wharton, a degree from Le Cordon Bleu, spoke fluent French, and loved to cook. In ordinary times he would have been the ideal choice for *Gourmet*, even though this was his first stint as a publisher. But these were not ordinary times.

"Is there anything I can do?" I was on my fourth glass of wine, feeling both earnest and sentimental. "I'd do anything to save the magazine."

He patted my arm. "I'll try to think of something."

The next morning I stood in the lobby, woozy and hungover, idly chatting with the editor of a fashion book while we waited for the elevator. "I've decided to elevate my personal profile in order to expand my book's reach," she said. My bark of laughter spiked my headache, but her words sounded so pompous. The woman whirled on me. "If you want to survive, sweetie, you'd better become a brand steward. Editor in chief is so last year."

That stopped me cold. I wasn't entirely sure how to be a brand steward, but, terrified by what was happening to our once-robust magazine, I was willing to learn. Since Giulio's departure, the revolving door had caused a precipitous decline in advertising, and as the ads vanished, editorial pages went with them. I could hardly believe the speed with which it happened, but each month there was less room for the articles we cared most about.

I stopped in to see Tom. "Would it help," I asked, "if I rolled out Brand Ruth?"

He gave me a huge, relieved smile.

THE TIMING WAS RIGHT. NICK had gone off to college, leaving me with a hollow, homesick feeling I could not shake. I'd expected to miss my son, but the depth of my devastation overwhelmed me.

"We only got to have him for such a short time," I moaned to Michael.

"He's not gone," Michael said, "he's just away for a while." Remembering my own relief at leaving home, I had a hard time believing this. When I left at sixteen, I was gone for good. Why would Nick be different?

"Because you're not your mother," Michael reminded me. "You're not crazy. He's not going to vanish. You'll see. But in the meantime you'll cope the same way you always do: by throwing yourself into your work."

He was right: It was what I'd always done and now that Nick was grown I regretted every minute I hadn't spent with him. I thought of all the nights I'd stayed late at the office, when I could have been at home. All the business trips I'd taken. All the client dinners. If I had it to do over again, I thought, I'd do it differently. But the time was gone, and it was never coming back.

I became the honorary chair for the Tenement Museum Gala, the Food Bank Gala, the March of Dimes Gala, the Great Chefs Dinner, the High Line Gala, the Who's Who of Food & Beverage in America.

"Thousands of press impressions!" said Karen, plunking a book fat with clippings onto my desk.

I went on the lecture circuit, staying up all night to research talks for Princeton, Columbia, the Radcliffe Institute for Advanced Studies, and the Oxford Symposium on Food.

"Thousands more press impressions!" Karen sang out.

I accepted awards: The Distinguished Journalism Award from the University of Missouri. The Matrix Award for Women in Media. The Genesis Award from the Humane Society. These too came festooned with media attention.

Tom was thrilled. When a clue in the *New York Times* Sunday crossword puzzle was "Food writer Ruth," he reprinted the puzzle and sent it to clients with this note: "*Gourmet*'s editor in chief is a household name."

But becoming my own personal publicity machine did not make me happy. I loathed the constant self-promotion, and I hated the way it took me away from the magazine for increasingly long periods of time. These days it was Doc who met with writers and edited copy. Larry sent messages about personnel decisions and Richard emailed layouts, but I felt divorced from the day-to-day life of the magazine. In a crisis they called, but all the things I'd loved best about being the editor of *Gourmet* now happened around me. Even when I was at 4 Times Square, most of my time was devoted to ad sales and corporate meetings. I began dreading going into the office, and I thought about Paul Bocuse's famous response when a reporter asked who did the cooking when the great chef was away. "The same person who cooks when I'm here," Bocuse replied. It had always seemed like a reasonable answer, but now I wondered if it made him as miserable as it was making me.

I began to notice the staff eyeing me warily, shooting me anguished looks. They understood that I'd fallen out of love with my job. Finally Sertl just came right out and baldly asked the question on everyone's mind: "Are you planning to leave?"

Appalled that my unhappiness was that obvious, I struggled to come up with a reassuring answer. Larry beat me to it. "Ruth's not going anywhere," he said. I waited for the zinger that was sure to follow; in one unforgettable exchange Larry had declared, "You're not nearly as nice as you think you are." What was he going to say now?

"She might want to leave, but she won't. She knows we'd all be in trouble, and Ruth wouldn't do that to us."

I stared at him in astonishment. It was the kindest thing he'd ever said. He grew pink with embarrassment and added a coda.

"Besides, she can't afford to. She has a kid to put through college." The laughter that followed was relieved; everybody knew it was the truth.

Ads continued to decline. Jobs were frozen. The paper quality went down. "I'm sorry I couldn't do a better job for you," said Tom when they brought in yet another new publisher. His prediction had been correct: The recession was grimmer than anyone anticipated, and *Gourmet* suffered more than most. Tom's replacement, Nancy Berger-Cardone, smiled brightly each month as she offered optimistic estimates of the number of ad pages she was certain to sell. And each month, still smiling, Nancy was forced to admit that the numbers were not what she'd hoped. There were no smiles on our side as we grimly tore the book apart, ripping out enough editorial pages to meet the shortfall. It was devastating to watch *Gourmet* dwindle, growing thinner every month. "It's not the magazine of good living," Doc said grimly, "it's the pamphlet of good living."

"Layoffs will be next," Larry said sourly.

Karen, ever cheerful, came up with yet another way to raise *Gourmet*'s profile. "We'll auction you off for charity dinners. If you go for enough money, it will be news."

"More publicity?" asked Michael as he watched me dress for the first of these dinners. "Is it really worth it?"

"These people paid a lot of money," I said. "And it's for a good cause."

"Are they interesting, at least?"

I tried to remember. "It's some Wall Street guy, his wife, and their friends. We're going to Craftsteak; Tom Colicchio donated dinner."

"Are you sure you don't want me to come along?" It was a noble gesture; Michael would be miserable at such an event. "Just to lend you support?"

"I appreciate the offer," I said, "but you'd hate it."

That was surely true. They were beautiful, these people who'd bought me, tanned, toned, and wrapped in expensive clothing. Their teeth gleamed, their jewels winked, and their hair glistened in colors unknown in nature.

The food was good, the talk polite. They asked endless questions about *Gourmet*, and I did my best to entertain them with amusing anecdotes about the magazine. I thought we were swimming along quite nicely until the man on my left threw down his fork and tossed me an angry glare. "You haven't asked me a single question," he snapped, "and I'm a lot more interesting than you are."

I looked at him, stung. "I'm sorry to be a disappointment. But you're the one who bought dinner with me."

"It's your loss," he replied, turning away.

Going home, I replayed the moment over and over, the way you can't help touching a sore tooth. It made me wince every time. I thought about what Stevie would have done with that dinner, how he would have delighted in asking questions, getting their stories, adding them to his address book. I scrolled through my messages, looking for the man's name, and googled him. Then I just sat there, staring at the screen: I was an idiot.

Ashamed and embarrassed, I crept into bed, hoping Michael was asleep. But he sensed my distress and came instantly awake.

"What's wrong?"

I groaned. "I was seated next to one of the most interesting figures on Wall Street and all I did was talk about myself. Brand Ruth might be good for *Gourmet*, but she's turned me into an obnoxious fathead who believes her own press. I should have asked Bill Ackman a million questions."

"Who's Bill Ackman?"

"You know, that hedge-fund guy who's always feuding with

everyone. He gives money to good causes and he's a fascinating man, but I was so full of myself that I blew the chance to get to know him."

"Well, he *wanted* to be there. You didn't."

"That's no excuse! Until I turned myself into a publicity machine I would have been eager to find out all about him, even if he was a jerk. He said it was my loss, and he's right. Brand Ruth may be good for the magazine, but I don't think very much of her."

The next day my publisher came up with yet another way to market Brand Ruth: Nancy persuaded American Airlines to sponsor a second television show. The shooting schedule would mean being away from the magazine for months at a time, which did not make me happy. But the deal was worth more than a million dollars to our bottom line, and there was no way I could possibly refuse.

As Nancy's team wrangled celebrities—Dianne Wiest, Jeffrey Wright, Tom Skerritt, Lorraine Bracco—I grew increasingly apprehensive. We'd be traveling the world on cooking adventures, and I worried that these divas would be impossible to please. By the time I left to shoot the first episode with Frances McDormand, I had worked myself into a state of high anxiety.

It did not begin well. The movie star frowned while examining her palatial suite at Blackberry Farm in the Great Smoky Mountains, grumbling as she took in the enormous marble bathroom with its spacious dressing room and walk-in closets. She was openly displeased with the bedroom; she glared at the huge fireplace and seemed to consider the giant four-poster bed particularly offensive. The airy screened-in porch did not meet muster, and when she saw the little kitchen she snorted derisively. Whirling on the cameraman, who'd been filming the tour, Fran demanded, "Take me to your room. I want to see where you're staying."

Alan shot me an exasperated glance; what had she been expecting? Did she really think his room was going to be better? He gave a world-weary shrug, as if to say, "Celebrities," turned off the camera, and led her out the door.

He tried going for drama. "This is all mine!" he announced, attempting a sweeping gesture to fling his door open. The door creaked, opened a tiny crack, then stopped, blocked by a mountain of camera equipment.

"As I suspected!" Fran put her eye to the slit in the door, staring into the small, cramped room. "This is just wrong." She stamped her foot. "You have to switch rooms with me. I certainly don't need all that space and you can obviously use it."

Alan's face became a comical mixture of amazement and disbelief. "C'mon," she urged, "all you have to do is say yes. You know you're going to be working harder than I am." Then she saw my own face, which must have mirrored Alan's. "What?" she asked.

It was pure Fran. She likes to cook and came along on a lark, but our little show meant nothing to her. Nevertheless, she threw herself into the enterprise as if it was the most important assignment she'd ever accepted. Neither dirt nor heat nor rain fazed her. She picked peas and stuck her hands deep into the dirt, crowing when she came up with handfuls of potatoes. The day we went fishing, she waded hip-deep into the stream, shouting with delight when she caught a trout (and laughing even harder when I caught a tree). Faced with a swarm of bees, she stood very still while they dive-bombed her head, then dipped a curious finger into the honeycomb, put it in her mouth, and grinned.

Fran was the anti-diva, so contrary to anyone's idea of a movie star that we all forgot she was famous. Only later, as we dashed through the airport on our way home, was I reminded that Fran is a solid-gold celebrity: People stared openly, their mouths agape.

When we heaved ourselves into our seats—we'd made the plane by seconds—the woman across the aisle fixed her eyes on Fran, refusing to remove them for a single second. Fran calmly ignored this until the woman leaned across the aisle to hiss in my ear, "Is that Frances McDormand?"

I nodded.

The woman scrabbled in her purse, looking for pen and paper. "Autograph!" she demanded, thrusting them at Fran.

Fran frowned down at the paper for so long I thought she was going to refuse. At last she accepted the pen. "I'm just an actor, and no more interesting than you are." She scribbled her name. "Probably not as interesting, actually. You should pay more attention to yourself and less to people like me. You'll be better off that way."

And that, I thought, is the secret to happiness: There is no Brand Fran. Suddenly I knew exactly what I had to do. It was time to shrink my profile. *Gourmet* would have to make do with plain old Ruth.

28

MIDNIGHT IN PARIS

WALL STREET WAS IN TURMOIL; PEOPLE WERE LOSING THEIR HOMES, unemployment rising higher every day. The stock market crashed. Newsstand sales plummeted—people give up magazines when times are tough—and we racked our brains trying to dream up an issue that people could not pass up.

"What about Paris?" I suggested. "The last Paris issue flew off the newsstand."

"And who"—Larry's voice was dry—"can afford to go to Paris these days?"

I thought of myself at seventeen, sleeping in a tiny room, wandering the streets, happy on little more than bread and cheese. "What if we did Paris on a shoestring?"

Doc interrupted my reverie. "Do you really think *Gourmet* readers want to go to Paris and pinch pennies?"

"You don't need money to fall in love with Paris. Think about Hemingway's moveable feast: It had nothing to do with luxury.

This could be the perfect moment to remind readers of the other side of the city."

"I see your point." Doc seemed to warm to the idea. "Nostalgia sells. . . ."

Larry remained unmoved. "And who, exactly, is going to write this story? I can hear the phone call now. 'Here's a couple hundred bucks; buy yourself an economy ticket, stay in a cheap hotel, and drink rotgut in the park.' How are you going to find a writer who wants to do that?"

"I'll do it!" I'd had no idea I was going to say that until the words had left my mouth.

Larry stared at me, incredulous. "Oh, come on!" He was at his most scathing. "You're not a Berkeley hippie anymore. Can you even remember the last time you flew economy? Do you really think you're going to enjoy sleeping on lumpy mattresses and eating in bargain bistros?"

I thought of Fran. I thought of Truman. "I guess I'll find out," I replied.

When we called our Paris correspondent, he was wildly enthusiastic about the idea. "Your timing is perfect!" cried Alec Lobrano. "There's a new energy here. Young chefs are moving out to the double-digit arrondissements—the tenth, eleventh, and twelfth—to keep costs down. The most interesting new restaurants are in the old working-class areas of Belleville and along the Canal Saint-Martin. Even the old *bouillons* like Chartier, who've been serving solid cheap food since the days of Toulouse-Lautrec, are hot again. Right now you can eat very well on practically nothing."

"I'm sure you can. And that's fine," Bill Sertl interjected. "But what about sleeping well? Paris hotels are expensive. Do you really think you can find an economy hotel good enough for *Gourmet* readers?"

"Probably not," I replied. "But I bet you can."

"You want me to come with you?" He sounded slightly appalled.

"Why not?" I said. "It'll be fun!"

THE MANAGER OF MY FIRST hotel had to shout over the blare of the television as she handed me a key. A brusque Brazilian, she had none of the edgy obsequiousness found at more fashionable addresses. "There's an elevator, but . . ." She peered across the high counter separating us, pushing stacks of paper to one side so she could study my small suitcase. "You would be wise to take the stairs."

Wise? Unable to resist the challenge, I wedged myself into the antique elevator, worrying as it wheezed slowly upward, stopping every few seconds to catch its breath. I imagined the chain breaking, the fall. . . . Relieved when it finally shuddered to a halt, I stepped into a narrow hallway carpeted in dingy gray, hoisted my suitcase over a pile of sheets, and squeezed past an abandoned vacuum cleaner. The door to my room creaked open to reveal a spartan space whose lone window looked onto an air shaft. The bathroom was just big enough to turn around in, the towels were thin as washcloths, and the sink held a single minuscule bar of soap. At least it was clean.

I sat down on the bed, which groaned beneath my weight, and felt the mattress. Larry, I thought, would be pleased: It was definitely lumpy. An image of the room at Le Meurice flashed through my mind; you could fit a dozen of these in there—and still have space to spare. I changed my clothes, splashed water on my face, and went off to meet Sertl. This time I took the stairs.

"How's your hotel?" We were walking through the eerily deserted streets of a remote residential district. Doors were closed, shutters drawn; even the lampposts seemed to shrink from us. This was not tourist Paris.

Sertl made a face. "Not exactly the George Cinq. The bathroom's down a flight of stairs, and if you want to take a bath you have to request the key from an unkempt gentleman at the desk who grumbles loudly about having to rise from his chair. I think I'm too old for forty-five-euro hotels in squalid neighborhoods. And our readers would hate it." He peered gloomily down the empty street. "Are you sure you've got the address right? We haven't passed a single restaurant."

"Pretty sure." But I was beginning to get nervous; the metro station was blocks behind us. Had I misunderstood the directions? "I think it's just around the corner. Alec said this was the best cheap meal in the city, and I guess you can't expect convenience when you're paying twenty-five bucks for a three-course dinner."

We walked on. With each block the neighborhood became less prosperous. The restaurant, when we finally found it, was small and spare, with bare wooden tables and hard wooden chairs. The waitress took one look at our unhappy faces and relieved us of our coats. "Did you think you were lost?" Her entire face turned into a welcoming smile and she hurried off, returning with an enormous ceramic terrine filled with game pâté, a plate of cornichons, and a basket of bread. She gave Bill's shoulder a motherly pat. "This should revive you."

I tore off a hunk of bread and scooped up a slab of pâté. The flavor filled my mouth—strong, rustic, a pâté with conviction. "God, this is good." As I took a bite of the crisp, salty pickle, I had a quick taste memory of the working-class France I'd known before my three-star days. I pushed the terrine toward Bill.

The air was filled with the soft melodic thrum of French, its cadence a kind of music. From the kitchen came the comforting thunk of pans and the scent of roasting meat, onions in butter, a hint of thyme. The wine was young, slightly sharp, but well made. The waitress kept our glasses filled.

The food was simple but very fine: a pile of petit gris, the tiny shrimp you find only in France, still in their shells. Fat white asparagus, simply steamed and drenched in sweet butter. A plump roast chicken with fresh morels and a sauce made of cream so rich it gleamed like gold. A handful of tiny strawberries, a cloud of chantilly, a wedge of Brie.

I sighed—I hadn't meant to—and Bill studied my face. "Maybe," he said, "you can go home again after all."

"We'll see," I said. "Our lumpy beds await us."

But when I opened the door to my austere little room, I threw the window wide, breathing in the air of Paris. In the tiny space between two buildings, I could just make out the moon. I slept without dreaming, and in the morning a plump maid in a blue apron knocked on the door and, with work-reddened hands, offered me a slightly cracked bowl of café au lait. On the tray were two croissants, a square of butter, a dish of apricot jam. I ate greedily, splashed water on my face, and walked out into the lovely light of early spring.

The hotel was at the foot of the rue Mouffetard, one of my favorite market streets; today the air smelled like strawberries. The stalls were filled with bright-green watercress, mesclun, frisée, and leaves of mâche. Fat spears of asparagus poked up their heads with such a curiously aggressive air I could not resist them. Munching the raw stalks, I stood at the fishmonger, admiring a big floppy turbot, a pair of eels, small, shiny rougets spread across oceans of ice.

In the bakery next door, people were queuing for croissants, and I looked into the window as a small boy stuffed an entire brioche into his mouth. A few doors down, a woman rushed out of the cheese shop, and as she careened into me I caught the fine scent of ripe Camembert, that seductive mixture of mushroom, yeast, and cream. Church bells began to ring. No meetings, no ad sales: The day stretched invitingly before me.

Bill was standing at the top of the street, looking so disgruntled that I did not ask how he had slept. "Tonight's hotel is bound to be better." I tried to soothe him as we meandered down the hill into the university district.

"It had better be," he replied morosely. "Changing hotels every night is hard enough when you're staying in great places. But this—" He stopped talking to stare, transfixed, at a menu tacked to a bright-green shutter.

"What is it?" I asked.

"A three-course menu for only twelve euros."

I headed for the door. "We have to try it."

"No!" Bill hung back, reluctant. "You know it's going to be like the hotel I just left: too small, too noisy, and very uncomfortable."

"What do we have to lose? It's barely noon. We can always have a second lunch. And a third."

As we stood outside arguing, the waitress pounced. *"Venez, venez, vous ne le regretterez pas,"* she said, herding us inexorably into the small restaurant.

She handed Bill the wine list. He handed it back. "Just water, please." I watched as a curiously avid expression crossed the woman's face. What could it mean?

"Je vous propose . . ." she began, with the French waiter's classic opening line. Mid-sentence, she stopped herself and snatched the menus from our hands. "I will bring you lunch," she announced. "You will be happy. *Ça va?*"

It was not really a question.

"Accras de poisson!" she sang out, setting fragile little fish fritters on the table. "I brought also the compote of tomatoes." She set another dish down. "You must, simply must, taste this. The chef makes even the balsamic vinegar himself."

Next she offered a plate containing two fluffy clouds. *"Cervelle de veau."* She said the words with great pride and watched us take the first bites, her mouth turned up in a small, satisfied smile. It seemed impossible that anyone had managed to coax calf's brains into this airy substance. "Christophe seeks out his own special suppliers," she said proudly. "He uses nothing but the best. You know he used to work with three-star chef Anne-Sophie Pic."

"Are you sure the menu said twelve euros?" I whispered to Bill; the waitress was now heading toward us, bearing a platter of hanger steaks. Setting it down, she forked meat onto our plates, then added a pile of chickpea pancakes. "Nobody, but nobody, makes panisses like Christophe," she said happily.

I looked at Bill. "Have you ever read the M.F.K. Fisher story that begins, 'That early spring I met a young servant in northern Burgundy who was almost fanatical about food, like a medieval woman possessed by the devil'?"

"No."

"It's about a waitress who takes such pride in her chef that at one point she says, 'Any trout is glad, truly glad, to be prepared by Monsieur Paul.' The food is superb, but as course follows course, Fisher begins to fear for her life."

The restaurant was starting to fill up, and Bill looked over at the waitress as she stood at a nearby table, decanting a bottle of wine with quick economical gestures. "I think," he said speculatively, "that she watched us arguing over the menu and decided we must be impoverished tourists, counting our pennies. When we declined wine, she knew she was right. She's proud of her chef, proud of French food, and this is a private act of patriotism. She's trying to seduce us with food. I haven't had this experience in years, but it used to happen all the time when I was hitchhiking around Europe."

"I remember that!" I was thinking of a meal in a small restaurant in Florence when I was twenty and another in Tours a few years later. People would lean in to tell me what to order and to share their favorite dishes. And every once in a while a chef would simply start feeding me, a point of pride because I was so new to the food. It was a generosity that was not reserved for restaurants. Once, stranded at Heathrow because of a canceled connection, the girl who'd been sitting next to me on the plane took me home to stay with her family. They were lovely people with a large house in Wimbledon, and I ended up staying a few days. Those things never happen when you travel on the excess express. The more stars in your itinerary, the less likely you are to find the real life of another country. I'd forgotten how money becomes a barrier insulating you from ordinary life.

Later, as I was writing about Paris, I wished there was some way to tell that waitress how her generosity had changed our trip. She'd opened the door to the Paris we'd forgotten, reminded us how it felt to be young, hopeful, and open to possibility. Reminded us how exciting it was to abandon security and run toward the life that is waiting.

After that lunch, Bill threw himself into the adventure, gleefully seeking out bargains everywhere we went. He discovered that entrance fees were waived if we waited to visit museums late in the day. He found free concerts in small churches and free food samples in department stores. And now every ride on the metro was another opportunity to meet strangers.

I kept wishing Michael was with me—he'd never seen this side of Paris—and I longed to share it with Nick. Bill missed his family too; each time he came upon some quaint architectural detail, he lamented that his partner wasn't there to see it. But we also understood that in some strange way we'd each found the perfect companion for this particular adventure. We'd both traveled light when we were young, and relearning how to live on very little was like flexing old, underused muscles.

Bill, more outgoing than I, had no qualms about stopping people on the street to ask for advice. Everyone was eager to tell us about a great shop, to point out a painting in the parish church, or to lead us to a local wine shop where generous tastes were poured. And every Frenchman had a secret restaurant we simply should not miss. We were rarely disappointed.

Our only failure was hotels. We slept all over the city, moving every night, but the cheap hotels were pretty awful. I'd been happy with my first hotel, but when Bill insisted on staying there himself one night, he was disappointed. "*Gourmet* readers," he said, "require more charm."

We did, finally, find one great bargain. The Hôtel des Grandes Écoles was so charming and so cheap it was *complet*—every room reserved for the foreseeable future. When I managed to snag a last-minute cancellation, Sertl was overjoyed. Mission accomplished. For me it was something else.

"The room was lovely," I conceded the next morning as we meandered along the Seine, "but I wish you'd been the one who stayed there. You would have appreciated all the amenities, and I realized I just don't care. As far as I'm concerned, a swell room means you end up spending too much time there, and I'd rather be out in the streets."

But Sertl wasn't listening. He had stopped before an ornately gilded window, and his nose was pressed against the thick leaded glass.

"We can't eat here!" I protested. "It's way beyond our means. This is the oldest restaurant in Paris."

"I know it is." He pointed to the menu tacked next to the window. "But they have a thirty-five-euro lunch special—and it includes wine. I've always longed to see the inside of Lapérouse. Haven't you?"

He had me there. The restaurant has been in the same place

since 1766, and through all those years it has remained un-changed. Of course I wanted to see the inside. "But . . ." I was hesitant. "The food's going to be dreadful. When I first came to Paris, Lapérouse had three Michelin stars, and over the years they've lost every one."

Sertl, however, was already inside the door.

The maître d' did not betray by the flicker of an eyelash that we were not dressed for such a formal establishment. *"Une de nos salles privées, peut-être?"* he murmured, leading us up a narrow set of stairs into one of the restaurant's famous private rooms.

Charmingly antique and extremely intimate, the small cham-ber was clearly intended for trysts. I sank onto the velvet sofa that lounged along one wall, staring up at an antique chandelier. Be-hind me an old mirror reflected the Seine, filling the room with shifting watery light. "I read somewhere"—Sertl was touching the scarred old mirror—"that the courtesans used to test the qual-ity of the diamonds their patrons gave them by running them across the surface of the glass."

I was just reaching up to feel the mirror when a waiter ap-peared. I quickly snatched my hand away. "Is this a special occa-sion?" he asked. "An anniversary perhaps?"

"Indeed," Bill replied without a moment of hesitation. When the waiter inquired how many years of wedded bliss we had en-joyed, Bill shamelessly replied, "Thirty."

"Trente ans!" The waiter refilled our glasses. And refilled them again. And again.

Mushroom bisque arrived in a porcelain dish; in the center, an island of foie gras slowly melted into a sensuous puddle. Veal came surrounded by a garland of interwoven vegetables as deli-cate as a filigree necklace; tiny gnocchi were scattered through it like little pearls. "But this food is wonderful!" I cried. It was the last thing I'd expected.

Hours later, as the meal rolled to a close with coffee, minuscule pastries, homemade chocolates, and caramels, I looked over and said, "I really loved this meal." What I was thinking, however, was that it would not have tasted nearly as good if we'd come from dinner at Gagnaire.

ALEC INSISTED ON MAKING THE reservation for our final dinner. "I want you to leave Paris with a good taste in your mouth," he said, "and L'Ami Jean is perfect."

We plunged into a crowded, boisterous dining room, making our way through an aromatic swirl of wine, butter, and onions. Voices eddied around us in a happy babble. A jolt of laughter rocketed out of the kitchen.

We sat at a table the size of a postage stamp, neighbors tightly packed on either side, studying the menu. I wanted everything: soupe de poisson a l'ancienne, rabbit cooked in its own blood, or perhaps those langoustines at the next table, shimmering beneath a translucent sheet of pig skin.

My eyes went up to the man who had ordered it. He was sitting alone. Skin the color of porcelain. Silver hair, a bit too long. Pale-blue eyes and that long, disdainful nose. It had been nearly eight years, but he had not aged. Even his clothes, threadbare and elegant, seemed the same.

"You remember me!" He emitted a little cry of delight and I noticed, again, how sensual his lips were. He lifted the bottle sitting on his table. *"Ce n'est pas le Krug '66, mais ce n'est pas mal."* As he began to fill our glasses, a waiter hurried over, reproachfully seizing the bottle from his hand.

"Have the duck," my friend whispered as I studied the menu. "You have no such birds in America."

"Et mon ami?"

"The scallops are superb."

The food was extraordinary, the duck a mineral slab of meat, blood rare, with the wild taste of lakes and forests. Bill's scallops—still in their pretty pink shells—sizzled with butter, sending delicious whiffs of bacon, garlic, and thyme shooting across the table. As the meal progressed in a blur of flavor, I found myself eating with joyful abandon. The old gentleman's eyes were on me, and I remembered him saying that I reminded him of his wife, because I ate as if I were a guest to myself.

For one brief moment I imagined that Severine was sitting across from him. The room would be less frantic in that other time, and the scent of cigars would fill the air. He'd be watching his wife as he was watching me, appreciating her appetite.

"You must have the rice pudding." He pointed; it was on every table. Rich, creamy, scattered with dried apricots and raisins, it was an extraordinary concoction, a dish more of yesterday than today. As I scooped up a dollop of crème anglaise I said, "I am so happy to see you again. But surprised to find you here."

His eyebrow lifted in a question. I gestured around the raucous room. "This is hardly Caviar Kaspia."

"Ah." He steepled his hands. "How young you are." He stared at the pot of rice pudding, considering his words. "When you attain my age you will understand one of life's great secrets: Luxury is best appreciated in small portions. When it becomes routine it loses its allure."

I remember his face, and the heady scent of almonds and cherries, as he said those words. I remember the musical French voices that surrounded us. And each time, I am grateful to my mysterious friend, for he'd put everything I'd discovered on this trip into a few simple words.

29

THIS ONE'S ON ME

IN SEPTEMBER 2009 I RETURNED FROM LAOS—WHERE WE'D SHOT the last episode of the new television show, *Adventures with Ruth*—to find the advertising situation improved. "Lots happening," my publisher gushed in an email. "Lot of good news. New biz . . . big units . . . exclusive business."

"Is she shining me on?" I asked Larry.

"No." He actually smiled. "Things *are* better. Louisiana Tourism is spending its entire advertising budget with us, which is huge. But that's nothing compared to the Macy's coup."

Nancy had persuaded the retail giant to layer five covers on the December issue, each featuring a picture of a different Christmas cookie. Larry pulled out a mock-up, riffling the layers to demonstrate. "It gives them five times the ad space and us five times the revenue. We'll get press for it too; nobody's done anything like this before. And I'm sure those pop-up cookie shops we created helped sell the space."

The shops had been the inspiration of Richard and our special-projects editor, Jackie Terrebonne. "What if we sold our Christmas cookies?" they'd suggested one day. "Everybody likes cookies, but some people don't like to bake. We could donate the proceeds to charity."

Before long, Richard had designed clever display carts and elegant packaging. In the end they also invented a line of *Gourmet* Christmas-cookie cards, complete with recipes. Larry did the numbers. "It'll be a nice little revenue stream," he concluded.

We'd also managed, with great difficulty, to persuade the circulation people to include a subscription to the magazine with every copy of our huge new cookbook. It made the thirty-five-dollar cover price a serious bargain and was a painless way to increase *Gourmet*'s subscriber base. I left for the book tour as the first reviews were coming in, and I knew Si was going to be pleased; we would hit the bestseller list again. For once I left town with a happy heart.

A week into the tour I landed in Seattle, one of my favorite cities, and went to lunch with a reporter from the *Post-Intelligencer*. The interview had just begun when my phone began to ring. Tom Wallace's number floated onto my screen.

"Yes?" In my current mood, I expected more good news. Even when Tom said I was wanted in New York, I didn't get it.

"I have to be in Portland tomorrow, promoting the cookbook."

"Forget Portland," he said. "You're needed in New York."

"Is something wrong?"

"Just come back." His tone had turned ominous. "Be in the office tomorrow."

It finally dawned on me that this was the call I'd been anticipating for ten years: I was about to be fired. To my surprise there was no panic, only sadness. I hoped the next editor would not clean house and everyone would be safe, but for myself I felt no fear. It wouldn't last—I knew that—but in the moment what I felt mostly was relief.

Almost everything I'd cherished about my job had vanished, leaving me feeling like little more than a salesman. I'd always known I was just a visitor in Si's luxuryland, and the thrill of all those perks had faded. I told myself that I could do without the fancy hotels, the limos, and the clothing allowance; Paris had shown me that I didn't need them. Peering into the future, I thought how different my life was going to be without the people who made my life so easy: Robin, Karen, Mustafa. Then I reassured myself that I still had all the people who really mattered: Michael, Nick, Bob, a large group of wonderful friends. I reminded myself of all the books I still wanted to write. This, I repeated over and over, was going to be fine.

I took the red-eye to New York, sitting up all night, but when I got to the office Robin was looking even more ragged than I felt. "They want us all in the conference room at ten," she said.

"All of us?" I was stunned; I could hardly believe that Si was going to turn this into a public spectacle, fire me in front of my own staff. It did not seem like him; he was not a cruel man.

We filed in grimly and stood silently watching as Si strolled in among us. He was brief. "After long deliberation, we have decided to close *Gourmet*."

We looked at one another, uncomprehending. Close *Gourmet*? Surely we'd misunderstood. They could fire us all. Take the magazine in a new direction. But they could not shut down such a revered institution. A world without *Gourmet* was unimaginable.

"It's very sad," Si added.

"How soon do we need to be out of here?" I don't remember who shouted the question.

"That's immaterial." Si was at his most imperious, and for a moment we all relaxed; the end was not imminent. The closing, at least, would be slow, orderly, dignified. "Your key cards will work today," he continued. "And tomorrow. Until five P.M."

It was like a sucker punch; we hadn't seen it coming. Tomorrow? We had to be out tomorrow? Glances flew wildly around the room as we absorbed his meaning: It was immaterial to him. As far as Si was concerned, *Gourmet* was already gone.

"What about the December issue?" With its big units, its exclusive business, and its five covers, December was already at the printer.

"There will be no December issue."

Someone—who?—began to sob.

This seemed to galvanize Si. "Human Resources will be available to answer any questions." They were the last words I ever heard him say.

We stood, staring at the empty space where he had stood. Doc put his arms around me and I began to cry. My mind was not working, and I found it impossible to process the fact that *Gourmet,* a publication older than I, was dead. I'd fortified myself against the pain of being fired, but this was worse: They had murdered the magazine.

It was James Rodewald who broke the silence. He walked out of the conference room and into the glorified wine cellar he called an office, returning with an armful of bottles. "I've got hundreds," he said, "and we're not going to leave them a single drop."

We drank while the phones rang and people packed up a lifetime of possessions. Many had spent their entire careers at *Gourmet,* and a cloud of dismal unreality hung over the office.

Is death always like this? I wondered as I discovered the strange, enervating energy of endings. Light-headed and unable to eat, I raced through the office, trailed by Robin, who was fielding calls from every news outlet in the country.

"I have nothing to say," I kept telling her.

"They still want to talk to you," she insisted, dragging me back to the phone, where I repeated, over and over, "I don't know." It became a mantra as one reporter after another demanded to know why Condé Nast had closed *Gourmet*. I don't know, I don't know, I don't know. "Why *Gourmet* and not *Bon Appétit?*" they kept asking, and I could only repeat the answer.

"What did Si say?" they insisted, hungry for crumbs.

"That it is very sad."

"That's all?"

"Condé Nast is a privately held company. He doesn't need to explain himself to anyone. And certainly not to me."

I was exhausted, a little bit drunk, overwhelmed. Human Resources asked me to stay on for six more weeks to finish the book tour and launch the television show, and for some reason I said yes.

Later I wondered why I'd agreed to honor contracts that no longer concerned me, but the entire day is enclosed in a bubble of unreality. When the cookbook's editor, Rux Martin, called, begging me to attend a special dinner in Kansas City the following day, I said yes. Farmers had spent three months raising special chickens to celebrate the book, and as Rux pointed out, the chickens had already been slaughtered. Somehow, that made sense; it would be wrong to waste them.

The sky grew dark and evening approached. We were in a crazy collective state of inebriation, running in and out of one another's offices to hug and weep. When would we ever be together again? In a maudlin moment I shouted, "Everyone come to my house!" Then I turned to Robin.

"Call Mustafa and get enough cars for everyone. Si can afford it." It occurred to me, as we rode uptown in this last gasp of silly splendor, that I would probably never say those words again.

We stayed up most of the night, and when Mustafa arrived the next morning, I was hungover. "You haven't eaten anything," Michael said as he saw me off. "Promise you'll get something at the airport." He was deeply opposed to my going and felt bad that I had to do it alone. "I wish I could come with you," he repeated over and over again. "I don't know why you agreed to do this—it's not as if it's your book."

"It seems like the right thing to do. It would be rotten to run out on the publishers at this point. Houghton Mifflin agreed to Si's million-and-a-quarter advance, and this is certainly not their fault."

"Just take care of yourself." He looked so worried.

Mustafa wore the same expression, and he was almost speechless with chagrin. "I can't believe it," he said as he dropped me at Newark Airport. He stopped, searching for words. "I'll be waiting when you come back. You know I'll always be your driver."

I got out and stumbled around the airport in a daze. "Eat," I said to myself. "You promised that you'd eat." I walked into the little sandwich shop and rooted through the offerings, picking up a steak sandwich; maybe it would give me a needed jolt of energy. I went to the cash register, but as I pulled out my wallet the cashier shook her head.

"This one's on me," she said. "I loved that magazine. I'm really going to miss it."

EPILOGUE

THOSE WORDS WERE PROPHETIC: I MISSED THE MAGAZINE TERRIBLY. Just not in any of the ways I had anticipated.

Like every other Condé Nast editor, I'd let Si tie me up in golden strings. The money, the limos, and the clothing allowance were just the beginning: He kept us so thoroughly insulated from ordinary life that for ten years I never balanced a checkbook, made a reservation, or knew where I was meant to be at any given moment. Someone was always there to see to the quotidian details, and the job often seemed too comfortable to quit.

There were certainly times in those first few months that I trudged to the subway in the snow thinking wistfully of Mustafa's magic chariot. I hated every hour wasted on the phone arguing over health-insurance bills or simply being stuck on hold. And I'll admit that I occasionally longed to eat a three-star meal.

But I'd prepared myself for that; Paris had shown me how little those things really mattered. Before long the life I'd led at Condé Nast began to fade, until it seemed like a distant dream.

But I had not anticipated the fear. As the months passed, I began to think I might never get another job and we'd end up losing everything: our house, our car, our savings. I had dreams about being a bag lady.

What surprised me most was how much the solitude unnerved me. I had worked with people all my life and now, alone at the computer, I missed my colleagues with a pain that was nearly physical. I'd loved the collaborative nature of magazine-making, and the long solitary days at my desk were deeply depressing.

With that feeling came a terrible sense of failure. I loved my *Gourmet* family and felt that I had let them down. Sixty-five people I cared about had lost their jobs, and as the days wore on this feeling overwhelmed me.

The best antidote for sadness, I have always believed, is tackling something that you don't know how to do. Now I decided it was time to try my hand at fiction. But it was hopeless. I sat at my desk, staring at an empty screen, incapable of finding words. My family and friends gathered around me, offering solace, and I did what I have always done in times of crisis: I began to feed them. And in the kitchen I found comfort.

Then the *Gourmet* people started finding jobs. Doc went back to *Cook's Illustrated,* Richard became creative director of Coach, and Sertl took a chance on an Internet start-up. Larry, to nobody's surprise, was courted by half the publications at Condé Nast. But going back to simply counting beans no longer satisfied him, and he eventually went off to find his fortune as a writer. Meanwhile, Jane became an editor at *Martha Stewart Living,* and most of the cooks were snapped up by other epicurean magazines. Gina Marie opened a

baking business (she specializes in birthday cakes), and Robin became the reservationist at a famous restaurant. Life, in other words,
moved on. It was time for me to do that too.

Finally, haltingly, I began to write again. I was sitting at my
computer, lost in a made-up world, when Giulio called to say his
mother had passed away. He wanted to bequeath me her treasure
trove of old *Gourmets*. Did I want them?

I hesitated. The issues from my own *Gourmet* years stared
down from the bookshelf, but I could hardly bear to look at them.
Still, it was a sweet and generous offer and I could not figure out
how to turn him down. "I'd love your mother's magazines," I told
Giulio. I did not add that they were headed straight for the base-
ment.

But when the postman rang the bell, I couldn't fight the urge
to peek into the boxes, just to see what they contained. The top-
most issue sported a fine old Henry Stahlhut drawing on the cover.
I remembered this romantic cake, and it gave me a warm feeling,
like encountering an old friend after a long time apart.

I pulled out the next issue. And the next, unable to resist the
lure of those old drawings. Hours passed, and still I sat there,
magazines piling up around me.

Suddenly, there was the leaping swordfish. It was a very ancient issue—1946—but even after all this time the fish had the
vibrant panache that had called to me so long ago. Almost uncon-
sciously, I opened the magazine to "Night of Lobster" and found
myself, once again, on a midnight island off the coast of Maine,
the sky above me bright with stars. Once again I smelled the
ocean brine, the seaweed, felt damp sand beneath my feet. And I
remembered, as I read, just how it felt to be eight years old and
setting off on a great adventure.

I reached for the next issue. Stahlhut had drawn something

called "Chilean Paella," a ridiculously old-fashioned concoction surrounded by fussy little artichoke hearts stuffed with olives. But when I opened the magazine I was reminded of all the reasons I'd first treasured *Gourmet*. In September 1960, most Americans were happily sitting down to sturdy meals of meatloaf with mashed potatoes, but those early issues offered an alternate foodscape. Here were recipes for Indian dal, lasagna with handmade pasta, mushrooms stuffed with snails, empanadas, Viennese boiled beef, even home-brewed vinegar. It was an international cornucopia, and I thought, proudly, that the magazine had truly been a pioneer. Then I turned another page and found myself staring at a recipe for German apple pancakes. It had been years since I'd tasted this particular dish, but the memory was so sharply etched that I could literally taste it.

My family had only one ritual: dinner at Lüchow's, a Wagnerian opera of a restaurant that looked, even in the fifties, like it had sailed onto 14th Street sometime in the very distant past. Lüchow's was famous for its enormous size, its classic German food, and the towering Christmas tree that soared above the tables during the holiday season.

We dined there once a week all through my childhood. We went because it was an easy walk from our apartment. We went because it reminded Dad of home. But mostly we went because Mom, normally so indifferent to food, was in love with Lüchow's apple pancake. Over the years Dad and I sampled every dish on the menu; Mom never ordered anything but that pancake.

I had never thought of making it myself, but now, overcome by a desire for this taste of my childhood, I studied the recipe. I had everything I needed: apples, eggs, lemon, sugar.

There's something soothing about peeling apples, about the way they come whispering out of their skins. Slicing them is another pleasure, and I listened for the juicy crunch of the knife sliding through the flesh. I cut into a lemon, treasuring the scent of the aromatic oils as they flew into the air.

Soon the seductive aroma of apples melting into butter drew my family to the kitchen. Even the cats came, twining around our ankles as we opened the oven and pulled out the pan. The smell was so alluring that we burned our fingers snatching bites from the pan.

Then there was an awful silence. Finally Nick said, "Your mother really liked this?"

Looking at that sad concoction, I remembered the yaffy and how restaurant recipes always needed to be tweaked. In 1960 *Gourmet* had neither kitchens nor cooks.

"C'mon, Mom." Nick opened a bottle of wine (he's almost thirty now), and handed me a glass. "I'm sure you can figure this out."

I tried to remember. The Lüchow's pancake wasn't fat and puffy, like this *Gourmet* version, but svelte and elegant. I pictured Mom, saw her face begin to glow as the waiter doused the pancake with rum and set it on fire.

Working from memory, I began breaking eggs into a bowl. The batter should be thin: a lot of milk and just enough flour to frame the apples.

As the scent of melting butter filled the kitchen, Nick's partner, Monica, wordlessly began to peel more apples. Michael poured himself a glass of wine. Outside, the sun began to set, filling the sky with a blaze of pink and orange. Sam Cooke was singing as I heated up the skillet. We stood there, shimmying around the stove, waiting to see what would happen.

Sometimes you know, before the very first taste, when a recipe is right. When I slid that floppy crepe out of the skillet, it looked exactly like the one my mother used to love. I sprinkled it with sugar, rolled it up, then heated rum and struck a match.

The flames leapt up, and as they died I wished, for just a mo-ment, that my parents could be with us. They'd encouraged me to follow my passion—even though it was one they did not share. It's been a long and very satisfying journey.

I hope they know that.

GERMAN APPLE PANCAKE

• • •

2 tart cooking apples
  (Granny Smiths are good)
1 lemon
½ stick (4 tablespoons)
  unsalted butter
¼ cup brown sugar
½ teaspoon cinnamon
Small grating of nutmeg

3 eggs
¾ cup flour
Pinch of salt
1 tablespoon sugar
1 cup milk
Sugar for sprinkling
Rum or cognac (optional)

Peel the apples, core them, and slice them thinly. Shower them with about 2 tablespoons of lemon juice.

Melt half the butter (2 tablespoons) in a medium skillet, and stir in the brown sugar, cinnamon, and nutmeg. Add the apple slices and cook over medium-high heat for about 8 minutes, until they've become quite darkly caramelized and smell impossibly delicious. Remove them from the heat.

Meanwhile, beat the eggs. Gently whisk in the flour, salt, and sugar. Add the milk. The batter should be thin.

Melt a couple of teaspoons of butter in an 8-inch skillet, and when it's hot, pour in a third of a cup of batter, tilting the pan so that it covers the entire surface, making a thin crepe. Cook just until set, about 2 minutes.

Evenly distribute a third of the apples over the crepe, pour another third of a cup of batter over the apples, then turn the pancake (this is easiest if you have two pancake turners) and allow the bottom to brown. Turn out onto a large plate, sprinkle generously with sugar, and roll the pancake up like a jelly roll. Sprinkle with a bit more sugar and, if you like, a splash of lemon juice.

Repeat this until you have three plump rolled pancakes. If you want to flame your creations, lightly warm a few tablespoons of rum or cognac for each pancake in a pan, add the pancakes, spoon the liquor over the top, and set the pancakes on fire.

Serves 6

ACKNOWLEDGMENTS

Together again.

When the news came that Jonathan Gold had died, suddenly and far too young, the *Gourmet* group gathered to lend one another comfort. It amazes me that even after all this time, we're still a family. Looking at all those people I love, I was struck by how rare this is—and how fortunate I was to have had them along on the exhilarating adventure that was *Gourmet*. Nobody has ever had better, smarter, kinder, or more interesting colleagues.

Or more entertaining ones.

"Remember the time . . ." Sertl began, "when Jonathan was in Las Vegas doing a piece, and he kept calling in with those hilarious reports? One night he told me he'd watched a woman run her finger down the prices on the menu until she found the most expensive dish. 'I don't know what she expected,' he told me, 'but I think she was hoping for some beautiful sea creature. When the waiter whisked off the silver dome to reveal a huge, jiggly gray mass, she sat there, stunned, staring at an entire lobe of foie gras. Finally she said, in a tiny voice, "But . . . do you think I'm Hannibal Lecter?" ' "

"I remember that," I said, "although I always thought Jonathan invented the Lecter line. It made a better story."

"What I remember," Nanette Maxim, Jonathan's longtime editor, weighed in, "is that he asked if I would please call every day, just to make sure that he was writing."

"And what I remember," I said, "is that you did it."

It was pure *Gourmet:* We looked out for one another, and I am still endlessly grateful. "That was the last fun job," Richard said at one of our reunions, and I hugged the words to me, cherishing them. When all is said and done, that is what makes me proudest. We should all have fun at work.

It takes a village to make a magazine, and I admired almost everyone I worked with at *Gourmet*. It pains me to have left so many of them out of this narrative, but you can only include so many characters before a book becomes too crowded.

Some I feel especially bad about leaving out of the book, like Paul Grimes and Maggie Ruggiero, two fabulous cooks and stylists who made the *Gourmet* kitchen fun. Nanette Maxim, maybe the kindest person who has ever walked the earth. Adam Brent Houghtaling, another great Larry hire, who created gourmet .com. And the wonderful production people—Stephanie Stehofsky and Margie Dorrian, who were at *Gourmet* long before I got there and were endlessly patient with me. And director of public relations Jennifer Petrisko, who helped me weather the magazine's end.

There were assistants like Shannon Rogers, whom I would have given anything to be able to promote, if only we'd had an opening. And editors like Cheryl Brown who have gone on to fame and glory.

And although they didn't work on my side of the masthead, I

wish I could have mentioned two of the most astonishingly creative women I've been privileged to meet, Jane Grenier and Daria Fabian.

I could go on, calling out every one of the people who worked at *Gourmet*. They are, pretty much in chronological order:

Elaine Richard, Hobby Coudert, Amanda Agee, Gina Grant, Marina Ganter, Jason Best, Natalie Mikulski, Miranda Van Gelder, Gerald Asher, Alexis Touchet, Lori Walther Powell, Elizabeth Vought, Katy Massam, Shelton Wiseman, Alix Palley, Ruth Cousineau, Lauren Irwin, Andrea Arundell, Myrna Alvarado, Diane Keitt, Ellen Morrissey, Helen Cannavale, Flavia Schepmans, Stephanie Foley, Corky Pollan, Catherine Jones, Russell Day, Ellen Boyer, Shannon Rogers, Amy Mastrangelo, Ed Mann, Daniele Vauthy, Hollis Yungbliut, Linda Immediato, Begay Downes-Thomas, Melissa Roberts-Matar, Margo Leab, Robyn Maii, Nichol Nelson, Sofia Perez, Beth Kracklauer, Sam Frank, Paul Grimes, Lillian Chou, Carla Corteo, Leslie Porcelli, Marisa Robertson-Textor, Emily Votruba, Roopa Gona, Haley Thurshwell, Eric L. Hastie, Amy Koblenzer, Nanci Smith, Julia Garcia-Tobar, Megan M. Re, Adam Brent Houghtaling, Emma Jacob, Andrea Albin, Laurie Nelson, Gillian Berenson, Sari Lehrer, Christian Wright, Kate Winslow, Rebecca Peterson, Maggie Frank, Caroline Patience, Chris Dudley, Kay Chun, Vanessa Shyu, Azon Juan, Leah Price, Rebecca O'Connor, Erika Olveira, Christy Harrison, and Carolyn Coppersmith.

I've been equally fortunate in the people I now work with. My editor, Susan Kamil, stuck with me, cheering me on through endless drafts of this book. My agent, Kathy Robbins, was there too, and I am grateful not only for her extraordinary patience, but for the way she swooped in when the magazine closed to reassure me that everything was going to be fine. Thanks to her, it has been. Gina Centrello—the perfect example of a great woman boss—

gave me really valuable notes on leadership. And I've been very lucky in the other member of the *Plums* team, Clio Seraphim; she is young and talented and I can't wait to see what she'll do next.

Once again, the brilliant Susan Turner has made a beautiful book. My father would approve.

Kathy Lord and Loren Noveck are copy editors to equal the great John Haney, and I am so thankful for their meticulous work. They are living proof that without copy editors the world is a lesser, messier place.

This whole book is, of course, a thank-you to the late Si Newhouse, but it can't be said often enough. If only the world had more people cheering for excellence.

Thanks to my girl group—Lissa Doumani, Robin Green, Caryl Kim, Laurie Ochoa, Margy Rochlin, and Nancy Silverton—who listened to me moan about my manuscript as we ate our way around the world. Through Barcelona, Tokyo, London, Paris, and both Baja and Northern California, you kept me sane.

I am also grateful to my Spencertown friends—Betsy Hess, Peter Biskind, Emily Arnold McCully, and Liz Diggs—who make rural life delicious and thought-provoking.

But mostly, and forever, thanks to Michael and Nick: You always make me happy.

ABOUT THE AUTHOR

RUTH REICHL is the *New York Times* bestselling author of the memoirs *Tender at the Bone, Comfort Me with Apples, Garlic and Sapphires,* and *For You, Mom. Finally.;* the novel *Delicious!;* and, most recently, the cookbook *My Kitchen Year.* She was editor in chief of *Gourmet* magazine for ten years. Previously she was the restaurant critic for *The New York Times* and served as the food editor and restaurant critic for the *Los Angeles Times.* She has been honored with six James Beard Awards for her journalism, magazine feature writing, and criticism. She lives in upstate New York with her husband and two cats.

ruthreichl.com
Facebook.com/ruthreichlbooks
Twitter: @ruthreichl

ABOUT THE TYPE

This book was set in Baskerville, a typeface designed by John Baskerville (1706–75), an amateur printer and typefounder, and cut for him by John Handy in 1750. The type became popular again when the Lanston Monotype Corporation of London revived the classic roman face in 1923. The Mergenthaler Linotype Company in England and the United States cut a version of Baskerville in 1931, making it one of the most widely used typefaces today.